D0204700

Making Sense of Accounting Information

Making Sense of Accounting Information

A Practical Guide for Understanding Financial Reports and Their Use

Leon Haller

President
Leon Haller Associates
Financial Planning and Management Services
Cambridge, Massachusetts

VNR VAN NOSTRAND REINHOLD COMPANY
New York

Copyright © 1985 by Van Nostrand Reinhold Company Inc.

Library of Congress Catalog Card Number: 85-3134
ISBN: 0-442-23249-7

Manufactured in the United States of America

Published by Van Nostrand Reinhold Company Inc.
135 West 50th Street
New York, New York 10020

Van Nostrand Reinhold Company Limited
Molly Millars Lane
Wokingham, Berkshire RG11 2PY, England

Van Nostrand Reinhold
480 Latrobe Street
Melbourne, Victoria 3000, Australia

Macmillan of Canada
Division of Gage Publishing Limited
164 Commander Boulevard
Agincourt, Ontario M1S 3C7, Canada

15 14 13 12 11 10 9 8 7 6 5 4 3 2 1

Library of Congress Cataloging in Publication Data

Haller, Leon.
    Making sense of accounting information.

    Includes index.
    1. Financial statements. 2. Corporation reports.
I. Title.
HF5681.B2H265   1985   657'.33   85-3134
ISBN 0-442-23249-7

*To Pearson Hunt, friend and associate
whose stimulating thoughts have motivated
and often guided this project.*

PREFACE

Are you a confused shareholder? A manager or owner of a small growing business whose accountant cannot satisfactorily explain what he or she is doing? Or just one of the millions of educated people trying to make sense out of the foreign language of finance?

Now you have a short, readable book that presents the fundamental ideas of accounting and financial analysis in the context of familiar business transactions and environments. Now you will be better able to translate business problems and successes from accounting statements. You'll find it easier to use financial information and analytical reports and to ask the financial questions that you increasingly need to know for your business and investment decisions.

This guide does not require that you have studied accounting or business finance. Unlike most books which start with a series of accounting definitions, this work focuses on the familiar transactions of a business undertaking — the purchase and sales of products and services. The most important feature of the following pages is the full and practical explanation of the flow of resource and financing transactions that characterizes different types of business enterprises. Thus, this book explains accounting measurements and principles from the owners' and managers' questions — "what are the financial costs, flows and financing problems of my business," rather than from the somewhat narrower technical view of the accounting professional.

Significant too is the practical discussion of the overall business risk of an ongoing enterprise and the risk of the different investors. The subject of risk remains the underlying theme as accounting measurements and terminology are defined for the reader and common approaches to financial analysis described. Many illustrations are employed, from the familiar corner grocery store business to the dramatic bankruptcy of Braniff Airlines. All examples illustrate the practical concerns of managers, investors, and financial analysts which are of greatest interest and use to the readers.

The guiding principle of this book is that all business enterprise is involved in the *conversion* — the purchase and sale — of human and material resources. All conversion entails *risk* — the possibility that the sale of goods and services will not generate enough revenues to cover the cost of producing what was sold as well as the financing of the resources required to continue the business. In this context, the subject matter of the book is translated from the readers' common knowledge of business transactions to the special classification system of the accounting profession and to the analytic framework of the users, the managers, the creditors, and the owners or shareholders.

Part I discusses in nonfinancial terms the diverse aspects of resource conversion as well as their financing implications in different types of business activity. Part II presents the view of the accounting profession expressed in the purposes and methodology of measuring the conversion activities. Also discussed in detail are the standard accounting formats of profit and loss statements and balance sheets. This section uses and defines the formal language of accounting. The last section, Part III, introduces and explores the fundamental concepts of financial analysis used by the business and financial communities and taught in the classrooms.

LEON HALLER
Cambridge, Massachusetts

ACKNOWLEDGMENTS

Many years ago at the offices of Standard & Poor in New York City, my supervisors started me on the path of eventually writing this book. Neither they nor I knew that their guidance of my learning about securities analysis would lead to the development of the ideas in the following pages. More recently, I have been particularly indebted to the Cambridge Center for Adult Education for providing the opportunity to explore the subject of financial information in adult education classes. Teaching business finance at the School of Management, University of Massachusetts and Babson College also provided the experience to hone and present the essential themes of this book (financial information and analysis) before many bright and inquiring minds of men and women with little experience in the business world.

Colleagues and friends are owed many sincere thanks for their suggestions and constructive criticisms. I am especially grateful to Barbara Geary, a former student who sharpened my mind to many of the phrases and thoughts I had expressed in the manuscript. I also want to thank all my family and friends for their continuing support and encouragement for my writing adventures and other projects.

Once again, I find myself very appreciative of the efforts of Jean Saint Gelais who typed the manuscript and offered valuable praise and criticism, along with our fun of working together.

CONTENTS

Making Sense of Accounting Information

Part I
A Financial View of
the Use of Resources

1
FINANCIAL INFORMATION–
BASIS FOR DECISION MAKING

Financial information focuses on the measurement of economic transactions. In any economy — free market, state-controlled or mixed — economic activity is constantly measured. Economic policy makers use the resulting information to encourage changes in the flow of resources.

In the micro-economic setting of a business enterprise, owners and managers maintain financial records. These records measure the monetary value of resources involved in the various transactions resulting from their decision to use resources for their particular products and services.

It does not matter if decision makers work in state enterprises, private ones, or cooperative nonprofit businesses. As people and organizations implement their business objectives, they channel resources of skills, materials, and equipment to their activities and convert them into new goods and services of value to others. Regardless of whether the market value of the resources employed — costs of materials, skills, production equipment — and the financial value of the output are determined freely between buyer and seller, controlled by national or local law, or subsidized in obvious or subtle ways, any given activity involving purchases and sales can be "accounted for".

The *books* of an organization are used to record and segregate transactions. Financial statements drawn from them are usually presented in general formats which categorize and summarize values of resources used and received in a business activity. The books are the sources of financial information presented in the universal language of accounting terminology. Financial measurement of the effects of past business decisions are shown in them. Future investment decisions are highly influenced by them.

While measurements of the *conversion* of resources from purchase to sale by an entity is the subject of this book, the focus of the following pages addresses the business activity within the private, profit-oriented sector of our economy. In this market, sales transactions are explicit and market values of resource inputs and output are generally subject to competitive pricing. Business decisions reflect all the resource transactions leading up to the sale or transfer of products and services between buyers and sellers. Put aside for a moment the images of words such as *price, cost, income, assets,* and *liabilities* and let's look at the general pattern of transactions which comprise all business activity.

THE MEASURED TRANSACTIONS

All business entities acquire resources, both human and material, in order to produce the result of exchanging goods or services in a final transaction or sale. The local supermarket, for example, buys vegetables and canned goods from suppliers. These goods are then available to customers when they come to the store to buy food. However, operating the store requires other resources such as brooms for sweeping the floors; cash registers for storage of money, tabulation, and recording of sales; telephones; refrigeration equipment; shopping carts and shopping bags; and shelving. A lease for the space is another valuable resource. It grants exclusive use of the building to the owners of the supermarket during the term of the lease which may cover 5 or 10 years. Such stores often have a deli counter where various products have to be cut, weighed, wrapped, and priced. In addition to the owner or manager, other people work in the store stocking shelves, helping customers, ordering from suppliers, preparing advertisements, counting money, and performing many other jobs requiring varying levels of skills. All of their labor inputs are necessary for the ultimate sale of goods to the supermarket customer.

If you went to the local or regional bakery (factory) where bread and other products were made and sold daily to the supermarket, you would see baking supplies in the storage rooms, workers handling the bakery equipment, and others preparing orders from customers or loading delivery trucks. People working in the office might be making calls to suppliers or collecting bills owed by the customers. They would be checking receipts of delivery of supplies and keeping records of paid and unpaid bills. Sales people, often those who make deliveries, might be out on the road visiting new customers or checking to see that the old customers have full shelves with the bakery's products well displayed. They would be trying to sell more of their products or introduce new ones.

If you look at the shelves of your local supermarket you will see many new items that were not available five years ago. Most of these products have never been advertised on television or even in the newspapers. Manufacturers, suppliers, and retailers are constantly changing their mix of products by introducing new ones, or upgrading or dropping old ones, in order to meet the changing needs and interests of their customers. Each introduction of a new product involves the use of new resources and, most importantly the risk that the product will not be saleable or will have less appeal than expected by its producers.

At the bakery, the owners may be thinking about buying a new, expensive piece of baking equipment that will expand their production capacity as well as reduce energy costs and improve the quality of the baked goods. They face the problem of financing the purchase of this major production resource and will have to borrow money from their bank or a commercial financing organization. Their accountant and bookkeeper will organize the financial information that will help them show a lender the potential profitability of new sales and their ability to repay the loan.

On the other hand these bakers, like many business owners and managers, have to decide if their products will be sold on credit, how much credit they will give a customer, and the terms of payment. The bakers, as a supplier to the supermarkets, are an important source of financing of the products that the markets sell. Financing through suppliers, derived from the delayed payment, enables the retailer to stock the shelves by using the seller's money. The credit arising from the delay in payment is effectively a short-term loan from the seller to acquire and use the seller's resources.

When customers don't pay on time, or do not pay at all, the bakers have additional work to do collecting the bills for the baked goods they have sold. They have their own obligations to pay their employees for their skills and their suppliers for other resources. In the normal course of the baking business, as in other business activities, employees are paid for the work they do, or the skills they

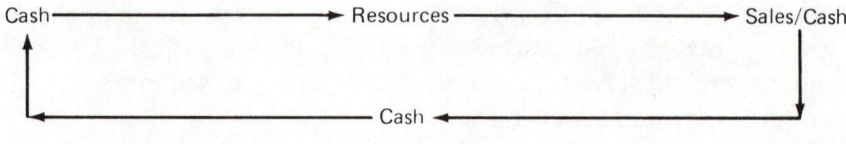

Figure 1–1.

possess. Whether the baker can sell the products they make or whether the customers pay their bills on time or at all is a separate matter, a separate contractual relationship. The same holds true in the business relationships with the suppliers of other resources or the commercial financing sources such as the banks. The flour milling company, one of the bakery's important resource suppliers, may make sales on credit to the bakery but it usually does not sell the flour purely on the possibility that the baked goods may be sold or that the bakery operators may be able to collect the cash from the sales. Insofar as resources are transferred from, or contracted through, a sale to a new organization or owner, the latter assumes the obligation to pay for them regardless of the outcome of the conversion cycle of the new owner.

In sum, while various businesses pursue different activities, all businesses share the same decision-making functions of acquiring resources, managing production, and selling the output of the products and services. The core equation or financial focus of all businesses is shown in Figure 1-1. If credit is used to purchase resources and to sell the final output then both ends of the equation are modified as in Figure 1-2 to show either or both.

The recoupment time is extended and the risk of the cycle is increased by the possibility that the buyer will not pay the obligation created by the sale.

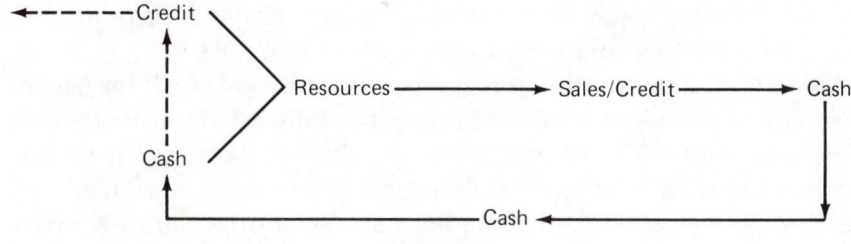

Figure 1–2.

Acquiring Human and Material Resources

Factory workers, cashiers, accountants, managers, sales people – all kinds of people provide different but essential skills to an enterprise. Services needed by all businesses include telephones; insurance for illness, fire or floods; garbage collection; and office and facilities maintenance. Material or tangible resources include those that will be converted from a raw state, i.e., eggs, flour, butter, vanilla, and sugar, to the finished goods such as the bakery products. Other forms of resources (production equipment, office supplies, etc.) are used up indirectly in the conversion. "Intangible" resources may also be involved. These could be patents, franchises, trade marks, or other exclusive rights to do or make something of possible value to some one other than their owners.

Converting Resources Into Saleable Products/Services

Managing production encompasses a wide range of activities from acquiring resources and skills to shaping or preparing them for final sale or transfer to a new owner. These conversion activities involve several functions including organizing the manufacturing processes or agriculture production, supervising and coordinating skills in various functions of production – ordering supplies, receiving them, scheduling production, quality control testing, storing, shipping, developing new products, etc. In addition, administrative support of the production activity usually requires many other skills such as training, keeping financial and other records, arranging financing, planning new products and dealing with safety or labor requirements.

Marketing/Selling the Output from the Resources Conversion

The word *marketing* includes an extensive array of activities with the purpose of making an organization's name known and selling its products. It also includes developing or finding different markets in which to sell. The extent of an enterprise's marketing efforts depends upon the nature of its output, the types of buyers and industries it sells to, and the size of its operations. Advertising is only one function, but a significant one relative to other activities, especially if the output is consumer-oriented. Advertising may be simple notice in a store window or local news weekly, or a broad and expensive TV campaign. It may include special displays, giveaways or discounts. Selling and marketing are done on many levels — to consumers, manufacturers, and other producers of new materials and services. Each enterprise is a buyer of resources that will be converted to output and sold to others. Each industry, indeed, each business, has different resource requirements for its marketing functions.

At the retail or consumer level, selling may take place in stores, door-to-door, by telephone, mail order, flea markets, or roadside stands. At the wholesale level, industry exhibits for gifts, hardware, machinery, computers, toys and many other items, bring buyers and sellers together annually in major cities throughout the world. Industry wholesalers and distributors are markets for individual manufacturers. Many markets are interrelated. The farmer grows wheat, sells it to the grain dealers who store and sell to other markets such as the flour mills. The latter sell flour to distributors who sell to retail stores for final resale to the consumer. If the flour is to be used by manufacturers of baked goods, it may be sold directly to the mill, to the manufacturer whose products are then sold to the retail stores, or to commercial food establishments.

Even the retail store sale to the consumer may be followed at a later time by a less formal resale of a used, unconsumed long-life product — a car, appliance, tool or hardware item. Unclaimed clothes left with the dry cleaner or abandoned possessions at moving and storage companies eventually find their way to new consumers or resale businesses. Other used products include antiques, along with coins, and postage stamps for collectors. These items, and many others, are bought by galleries, auction houses, and dealers for resale to new users.

2
FINANCING THE RESOURCES OF A BUSINESS ENTERPRISE

SHORT- AND LONG-LIFE RESOURCES

The activities noted in Chapter 1, and many more within each category, require payment for personal skills and services and for tangible resources used in the production of new products and services. Most business entities which sell their products and services provide credit for their sales transactions. They finance their customers' use of their products. The provision of credit is a common condition of most sales transactions in all markets.

The credit, from the sellers' point of view, delays payment of the obligation arising from the transfer of the output to new ownership. For the buyer, credit offers a method of financing the resources acquired which allows for a delay in the payment of cash for the resource transferred. Thus, the buyer may have some time to convert, or use the acquired resources before paying for them. In order to provide this credit, the seller must have adequate financing to act as a "banker" for the purchasers.

The local food store may buy the food it sells on credit, with expected payment before the next delivery or within three, seven, or ten days. The seller's decision to extend credit depends on the reputation of the buyer for paying bills, the perishability of the product, the popularity or expense of the item, and the payment terms of other sellers of the same or similar products. Items such as caviar and other gourmet foods may be sold with more generous credit terms than frozen corn or canned tomato sauce because, as luxury items, they move slowly from the shelf to the consumer.

Financing Short-Life Resources

The financing requirements of an enterprise reflect the cycle from cash and credit resource purchases to cash and credit sale of output.

The financing patterns vary according to the types of resources used, the credit available from the resource suppliers, the duration of the production cycle, and the time required for selling the output. To trace the economic activity that produced the pastry on the shelf of the supermarket one must start at the primary producer level. The farmer usually borrows funds to buy seed, fertilizer, and pesticides which will produce a crop several months later. The farmer, and particularly the workers, have to be paid on an ongoing basis for their work. Since their final product may not be sold for several months, or longer if the grain is stored for sale in the future, financing of the production cycle and storage time is required until the revenue-generating transaction is completed.

The worker in the flour mill may receive a weekly wage, but the flour that he or she helped to produce may have been sold on credit. The bill may not be collected for 60 days or more from the time when the wheat passed through the milling machine. If an indepedent wholesale distributor is involved in facilitating sales between the miller and the bakery customers, then a similar cycle of storage and sale on credit may be experienced in that enterprise. Chances are that a large miller would supply a considerable level of credit in financing the flour in a bakery supplies distribution business in order to facilitate sales.

At the bakery level, flour would probably move into and out of the bakery in the form of pastry and other baked goods fairly quickly. While credit would most likely be available to most of the baker's wholesale customers, it would be available only a relatively short time since the shelf life of the product is relatively short, and the customers are paying cash to the supermarket for the bakers' goods.

At the supermarket level, baked goods are purchased and sold every day. No credit is extended to the retail buyer and the financing cycle for the bakery products is relatively short.

If you consider the seasonal nature of most business activities, you often see a distinct gap between the payment for many resources used in the business and the receipts from sales of the output. A large part of the financing requirements of such businesses involves the short-term cycle of production (or production and sales credit) or such costs as storage, display, and possibly advertising associated

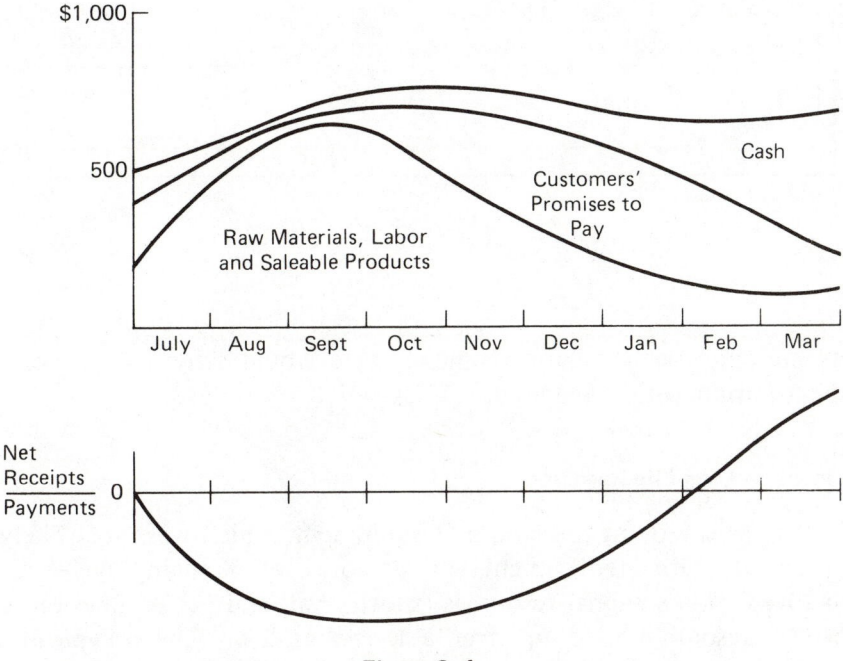

Figure 2-1.

with the sale. For example, the production of clothes that will be sold in the midst of winter by a department store is often begun by the manufacturer four to six months earlier when people are complaining about the heat.

The commercial banking system supplies the bulk of funds for short-term loans for economic phases of production, warehousing of goods, seasonal sales, and sales on credit. Graphically the resource financial flows for the production and sales of a seasonal production would most likely appear as shown in Figure 2-1.

The financing requirements of each level of economic activity involving the flour also reflects the use of other resources, i.e., farm machinery and land at the producer level, milling machines and storage facilities and delivery trucks at the processing level. Each level to a varying degree, requires office equipment such as desks, files, typewriters, and adding machines. If you assumed that the farmer rented the land and equipment each season, that is, paid for

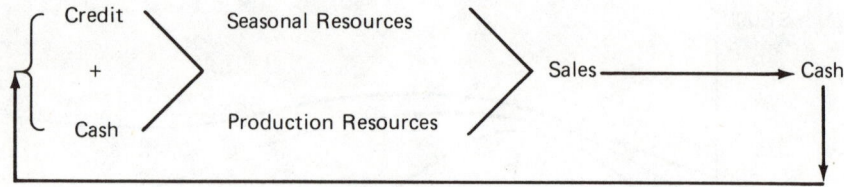

Figure 2–2.

its periodic use, then the financial cycle would essentially be of a short-term nature. (See Figure 2–2.)

Financing Long-Life Resources

If the farmer owns the land and equipment, which was most likely purchased with credit, then two categories of financing cycles are involved: (1) seasonal resources (short term) and (2) production or capital resources used up over a long period of time. Typically, credit for the latter reflects the *useful life* (or lives) of such resources. Large pieces of farm machinery may be financed over a 10-year period, and trucks over 5 years, because they can be productively used over those periods of time or longer. Land is typically financed over a period of 20 to 25 years. (See Figure 2–3.)

As an owner, the farmer's production resources, or rather a part of them, are used up in the annual production of the crops. Insofar as that part is recognized as part of the cost of production, it must be returned to the owner in the sale price of the output. The resource conversion cycle represented in the annual production and sale can provide the full refunding of the seasonal credit and the partial refunding of the credit for the long-use (production) resources.

The problem, from the creditors' perspective, is that the loan repayment schedule for long-use resources is based upon so many annual conversion cycles. In terms of the business risk, the questions are: "What are the possibilities that the market prices for output will not provide enough sales revenues to cover the annual cost of production?" "Will the borrower be able to make all the loan repayments plus the interest charges, or financing cost?" The short-term

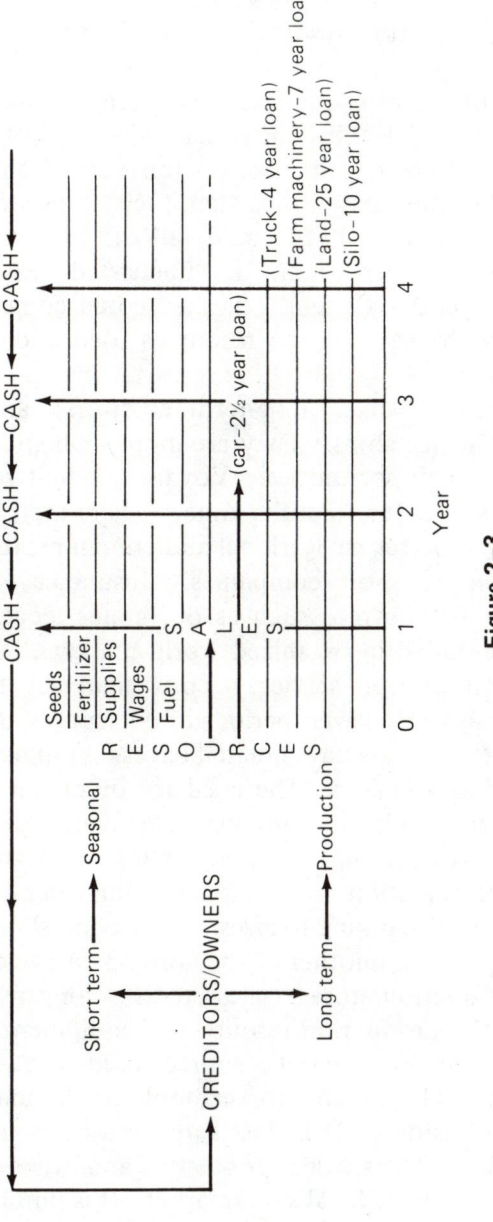

Figure 2–3.

lending for production, or for sales on credit, is less risky than a long-term loan for production resources used up over many production cycles or years.

In the fifteenth century, merchants financed the construction, crews, and supplies of trading ships that sailed out of Genoa. Their cycles of production or resource conversion were often three or more years. The risks, the possibilities that their ships would not come back, were tremendous. They could fall off the end of the earth, pirates could overpower them, the uncharted seas and weather conditions could destroy them. Or they could come back without a valuable cargo to pay for the resources used and to reward the merchant/investors.

Today, investors, banks, (long-term creditors), and government agencies often finance ships. They are more sophisticated about the industry costs and opportunities. Voyages of halfway around the world are made in a few months time. There aren't many pirates around, and much better navigational and communication equipment serves the ocean transport companies. Insurance is available for disasters. Most bulk cargos such as oil, grains, coal, and minerals are known and traded in organized world markets. Ships are hired purely for transportation service. You might say there is barely any risk these days. However, periods of oversupply of commodities such as oil in recent years have created excess shipping capacity built relative to previous demand. The need for oil tanker transportation has fallen and the capital or production resources (ships) that had been financed were not sold (rented) at high enough prices to pay for their costs of operation, including their financing.

While commercial banking focuses primarily on short-term lending to finance one phase or another of the conversion cycle — acquisition of resources/production/storage/sales credit — longer term financing is required for the production resources — equipment, facilities, and buildings. These are the *capital* resources used to make products or provide services. The tanker, for example, is the main resource of the oil shipping business. It is "used up" in or has an *operating life* of 15 to 20 years. The stock of food stuff and other consumables is the main resource of the local supermarket. It is purchased, sold and repurchased again usually in a very short period of time. Thus these two enterprises have main resource lives of opposite characteristics.

The retail food business uses or converts resources to cash very rapidly. It has a high resource turnover rate or cycle. The ocean transport business depends on the use of a very long lasting resource. Therefore the economic conversion of the ship into shipping services covers a lengthy cycle. It provides cash recoupment over time.

Each business has a different resource conversion cycle for its output. Furthermore, each business encounters a number of different cycles representing the types of resource used. Because the conversion cycles are different, the financing components can be of varied lengths — short-, medium- and long-term. As the tanker is chartered (rented) to oil shippers, its use generates revenues over many years which will pay for the resource costs incurred to produce it (the purchase price of the tanker), costs of the business activity, and financing costs of the tanker and other resources. Part of the annual cost of operating the tanker is a portion of the original cost of the tanker. It represents a partial "using up" of the resource. This cost, along with the regular operating costs of maintenance, the salaries of the captain and crew, insurance, the administrative costs of overall management and selling, and financing costs of annual interest charge on borrowed funds to buy the ship, sets the minimal basis for determining the rental fees for the shipping services.

The conversion cycle of the ship as with other capital equipment or facilities — airplanes, toll roads, buildings, specialized machinery, trucks, or railroad cars — occurs over periods of time which may vary from four or five to 25 or even 30 years. Consequently, these longer life resources are generally financed on a long-term basis relating to their specific conversion cycle. Figure 2–4 shows the financing cycle of a truck.

The initial purchase requires either owners' investment or a loan, or most likely, both. The annual cost of using up a piece of equipment, e.g., a truck with a four-year useful life would be a portion of its original cost. It must be calculated into the total annual cost of operating the truck in a business. Consequently, it must be included in the price charged for its output or use. As revenues come in from each year's production of trucking services, the original cash outlay would be returned to the financing sources.

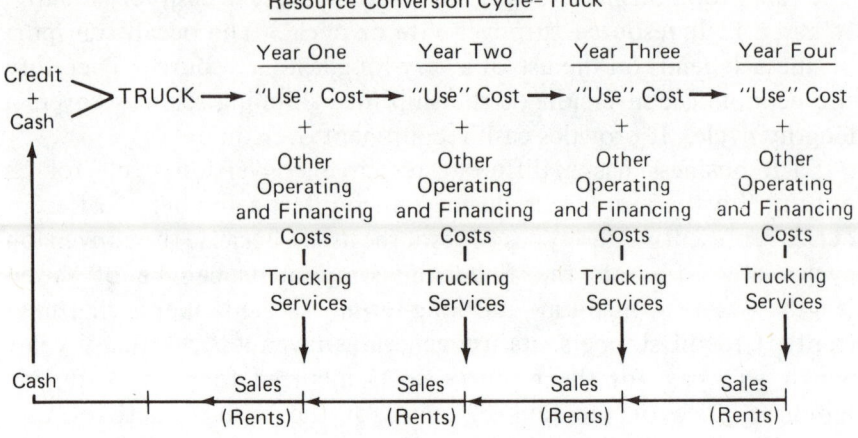

Figure 2–4.

THE FINANCING PERSPECTIVE

All lending is contractual. In exchange for the use of a given amount of funds, over a period of time, the borrower agrees to pay the lender a stipulated cost per year, which is an interest rate. The borrower also agrees to repay the loan at a given time or times. Other conditions and limitations on the borrower may apply in order to safeguard the lender's investment.

A lender's agreement usually sets specific terms of repayment. These terms of the credit relate to (1) the financial expectation about the productive life of the resource, and (2) the stability of the borrower's business. The latter pertains to the risks that the outlay for the resources expended at the beginning of the conversion cycle will not be recouped over time. Long-term lending agreements, such as bonds, are a chief source of financing for enterprises which purchase capital facilities and equipment. In many instances, the bondholders' investment is *secured* by the particular resource. That means the bondholder has a recognized legal interest or claim in the conversion of the resource until the loan is paid. Mortgages on buildings have the same characteristic. A mortgage loan is credit secured by a major physical resource. Bankers generally look for security or *collateral*, some type of valuable resource that backs the promise to repay a loan. Thus a car is collateral for an auto loan. A house may be used by an owner as collateral for a business loan. Collateral gives the lender the right to take possession of the resource if loan repayments from the owner are not forthcoming according to the agreement between lender and owner.

There are many kinds of long-term financing agreements — equipment loans, mortgage loans, revenue bonds, debentures (general credit), and production payout loans (oil and gas). Various mechanisms and conditions associated with these loans help safeguard the lenders' investment or control cash generated from the resource conversion activity of an enterprise. Commercial financing for equipment lending is available through banks and nonbanking organizations that provide business financing. Commercial banks will arrange shorter term loans, but long-term loans of 7 to 25 years for production facilities and real estate are generally financed by specialized savings and loan banks, insurance funds, corporate pension funds (institutional lenders) which invest in relatively secure long-term investment of a low-risk nature.

The cost of the borrowed funds sometimes includes an additional right to share in the owners' profits from the conversion of resources, especially if the conversion cycle is of a *high-risk* nature. This also occurs when there is a strong demand for loanable funds and a relative shortage among lenders. Thus, during economic periods of "tight" money (credit supply), long-term lenders have sometimes required special incentives of some type of ownership participation ("equity kicker") which they hope will provide them additional compensation above the contractual interest rate on their investment.

Interest rates and loan repayment terms reflect the risks of conversion of a particular business and the supply/demand conditions of loanable funds in our banking and financial institutions. The financing risk of a particular business operation pertains to the changing financial condition of a company and the priority of claims to the revenues generated by the use of the resources. These are expressed in the financial relationships among other lenders (secured and unsecured) and with owners. For the lenders, the level of owners' financial participation in the cycle provides a certain amount of security since the owners have the responsibility to repay their contractual loan obligations, regardless of the outcome of the cycle.

If money is "lost" in the conversion cycle, that is, if the output when sold provides less than the cost to produce it, the owners absorb the loss by using their funds to repay the loan. In general, the greater the owners' financing, the less the overall risk of the lenders.

Lenders are a source of *limited risk* financing. They make funds available for use by the borrower (owner) for a specific period of time. They are not interested in financing 100% of a business activity, since there is never any guarantee that the resource conversion cycle will be completed or that the borrowers will be able to fully repay their loan plus interest charges. As a practical matter, the owner would lose nothing if a business was fully financed by creditors. Lenders share to some degree the overall risk that the conversion cycle may not produce the revenues to repay the financing used in it. Of course, the greater the risk of not being able to repay, the higher the cost of borrowed funds and the less available the lenders' capital to an enterprise. Thus, when a business starts, owners have to provide a greater portion of the financing of the resource conversion cycle to pay for the resources used in the business. As demand for the output of a business grows, that is as the *market* for the output is demonstrated, the business activity becomes less risky. Likewise, as the ability of the owners to manage the resource conversion cycle grows, the business activity becomes less risky to potential sources of credit. More financing may be made available by suppliers since they will want to benefit from the growth and will feel more secure that their bills will be paid on time. Other lenders, particularly banks, will be interested in financing on terms which may be somewhat less restrictive to the managers of the conversion cycle and to the paying out of rewards to owners.

THE OWNERS' PERSPECTIVE

As implied in the previous discussions, sources of business financing comprise only two categories: lenders (or creditors) and owners. Different classes such as suppliers, bankers, and mortgagors, preferred and common owners within each category may share different levels of risks and rewards, but there are still only two categories. Owners may put their funds into an enterprise directly in the form of *shareholder* capital in a corporate form or as *partners* in the partnership relationship. Insofar as earnings from the activity (surplus from the conversion cycle) are left in the business — reinvested in resources rather than withdrawn from the cycle by the owners — they are also a source of ownership financing. As stated earlier, if losses occur in the conversion cycle of business, owners absorb them through a reduction of their invested capital and a reduction of the surplus previously accumulated in the business (if any).

Surpluses accrue to the owners as a result of their vision about using resources or some particular aspect of structuring the conversion cycle. Just as solving a problem in an operational sense uses resources and skills differently to achieve a different end result, business entrepreneurs attempt to acquire and develop resources to sell to users in different ways than commonly practiced. The range of marshalling the resources are innumerable. They may be simply opening a store where there was none before, introducing many new products in an established store, or inventing a new machine or product to satisfy an industrial use or meet a consumer need. Whether the product is "essential" to the life of the consumer is not important in the idea of "need." It is crucial however for value to be placed on the product through a sale, an exchange, which will be greater than the cost to produce that product by a given enterprise. A few years ago, a clever entrepreneur marketed a "pet rock" to many urban buyers who responded to the spoof on the nation's love for animals. The buyers gave the product "value" and rewarded the innovator with a small fortune. Value of resources is created in the exchange between seller and buyer.

OWNERS' SKILLS AND INVESTMENTS

Owners may often sell their skills as well as invest in the cycle of resource conversion activities of a business. An engineer may be a part owner of a company in which he or she will risk investment in the resource conversion, but also receive payment for the sale of engineering skills to the company. These different roles of skill-provider and financier can become so intertwined that they do not appear to be different. For example, when a person or a couple buy a small food store, they may draw an income (reward) for both their skills of running it and because they are the owners. Most management or operational skills are replaceable, therefore separable, from the investor role. Everyone has heard the approach of "I've got the brains (skills) and you've got the money; we'll go 50/50." Valuable or specialized skills are often part of an exchange for ownership, separate from the financing.

Typically, in the formation of new enterprises, owners do not receive a day's pay for a day's work of performing organizing, coordinating, and sales functions. They exchange the value of their services (salaries) for payment at a later date, or in fact contribute their work. Sometimes when new companies buy the skills of specialists, they offer an opportunity to "buy" ownership at a low price.

Computer specialists sometimes work for new firms for one-half to two-thirds of the salary they could receive in a more established enterprise. But in addition to their salary they also receive a right to buy, through stock options, an interest in the ownership at a later date at a low price. Consequently, the risk that profitable products and services from resource conversion will be effected by the company is partly borne by them along with other financing sources. If the company is successful, they could receive greater rewards through ownership, rather than just the current market value of their skills. If not successful, the company was able to employ their skills (resources) at a lower cash cost than the labor market value required at the time.

Acquiring resources by agreeing to share possible future conversion revenues is a common method of attracting special resources and financing them. Patents and other exclusive rights are often "sold" in the form of an exchange for a percentage of future sales or an owner's interest in an enterprise instead of outright purchase from the latter. Future payments such as royalties apply to the use of resources/over time and in relation to a volume of use such as the number of copies of a book sold, barrels of oil extracted, or tons of coal mined. Oil and mining companies buy leases, which are rights to extract what they find. The value of future finds is unknown. A lease with producing oil wells may have a much greater market value since the risk of finding oil has already been taken. In such cases, the business risk has more to do with how much oil is still in the ground, the cost of extracting it, and the future price which will be received for it. Information exists concerning past productivity and revenues. Estimated "reserves" of unextracted oil as well as the sales price from future output may be professionally calculated. Lenders are more likely to help finance the purchase of producing wells than a lease on unexplored property, unless their loans are secured by other valuable and productive resources.

Lending for a producing well as opposed to a new drilling provides a clear example of the participation in the lesser-risk part of financing the resources in a conversion cycle. Lenders receive a fixed interest payment for the use of their funds. They receive claims to the resources in relationship to the owners and in the distribution of the revenues generated from the conversion of the resources. Use of credit partially shifts the control of the conversion of resources from the owner to the lender. Thus, the ownership financing covers the greater risk.

In financial terms, owners' rewards derive from the risk of undertaking the conversion cycle. If a large pool of oil was discovered while drilling in a new and unknown place, revenues from the sales of the discovered oil may be calculated to be several times the cost of getting it out of the ground. Based on that expectation, a commercial loan from a bank for the well-completion equipment and possibly for storage or pipeline might be made. The full investment to extract the oil could be provided by both the owners and the bank, the latter portion based on cost of production resources needed and the expected value of the oil when it is sold. Thus, the conversion may yield a substantial surplus above cost and after the repayments have been made for the loan. The initial risk of the investors was whether they would find oil or not. With a loan, their ownership claims to the oil and the production equipment may become subordinate to, or subject to, the conditions of the lenders' agreements. Since the value of the oil found is expected to be greater than the cost to produce it, the mutual interests of the financing sources can be negotiated.

Suppose the price of the oil fell substantially, a condition which occurred in the latter part of 1982 and early 1983. The well which had been profitable for a year was now unable to produce enough revenue at a lower oil price to repay the loan. The value of the output, the oil, has changed. The resource conversion cycle no longer produces a surplus, or only a marginal one. If a substantial loan repayment was due, the owners would be unable to make it, and the bank would have a broken loan agreement and a loan in default. Without further investment from the owners to repay the loan, the lenders are faced with protecting their claims to the resources and ensuring recognition of their repayment priority in the sale of the resources of a discontinued conversion activity.

BANKRUPTCY

Stories about corporate bankruptcy usually start with the fact that a company has sustained severe losses and is unable to make payments to its creditors. Major lenders usually attempt to reschedule the debt. Such rescheduling involves redesigning the repayment schedules and amounts of the earlier loan agreements to coincide with revised expectations about the revenues from the company's future conversion cycle over time. Sometimes rescheduling is linked with the sale of specific resources such as buildings, product lines, and businesses within the company in order to reduce the total debt or its repayment to a manageable level. If this cannot be done, major lenders exercise their right to *call the loan*, usually a part of the lending agreement. The *call* is a formal request for full payment. It is a remedy of the lender when the borrower breaks the loan contract. It usually occurs when the owners' investment has been reduced by losses or is fully tied up in unsold resources. Through this right, the lender has considerable influence over the use of resources and revenues generated from them when the financial condition of a company is weak or the risk of the conversion is substantially shifted to the creditors.

Any one creditor may make this demand, so all creditors will be concerned that someone may be paid before them. Each is hesitant to push the button for fear of the collapse of the company. But when the demand is made, a company usually applies to the bankruptcy court for "protection" against the creditors while an attempt is made to work out a repayment plan. The protection through suspension of payments to creditors and the financial reorganization however is done under court supervision. Thus the resources and the distribution of revenues from them come under control of a third and independent party, the federal bankruptcy court. Creditors have to agree to a plan to settle their claims for loan repayments for the resources they have financed. Either a company's finances are reorganized and a plan of repayment approved by the creditors under a Chapter 11 bankruptcy proceeding, or the company is dissolved and the resources sold under a Chapter 10 proceeding. A business may operate under court review for several years, until its reorganization plans are fully implemented, debtors repaid in one form or another, and the prospects for the continuation of the business are strong.

When a company is dissolved and the resources sold (at auction to the public), the creditors face the probability of receiving a small fraction of the debt owed to them. Proceeds go first to satisfy past tax obligations, then to secured lenders, to unsecured lenders and last to owners, if anything is left. This sale is a forced conversion, which usually results in a poor recovery of cash. Therefore, it is usually not in the interest of the creditors to seek a dissolution of the operations of a business. The continuation of the enterprise may enable a recovery of the loan financing or part of it. The orientation of the court is to recognize and safeguard the interests of the creditors which, if business is economically viable, is best done through restructuring its operations and finances.

Lenders in their credit agreements with borrowers seek to protect themselves against the risks of conversion by (1) requiring substantial owners' financial participation directly invested in the business, and sometimes through personal guarantees of loans by owners with other nonbusiness resources, or the ownership shares themselves, or (2) securing the loan with a claim to specific resources of the business operation or (3) by both.

The larger the business enterprise, the more removed the owners tend to be from the decision making. Management becomes separate from ownership which is represented by a board of directors. Lending becomes less personally controlled or related to the acts of the owner/managers and only the resources of the organization are subject to use as collateral.

The financing structure of an individual enterprise typically reflects the mix of short- and long-life resources. Thus, the financing for a supermarket operation is usually heavily dependent on suppliers' credit and other short-term financing. A shipping company relies on the long-term financing from bondholders whose security is the ships that are financed. Of course the percentage of owners' financing of the total amount of resources used in the conversion cycle will vary according to the risks involved in the conversion in the particular type of business or industry. The risk measurement may also include the reputation of the managers/owners for their ability to sell the products and services and pay bills on time, especially where smaller companies are involved.

In summary, all business activity can be seen as a grouping of functions which compose resource conversion and their counterpart financing cycles:

	1) Acquiring human and material resources	Financing
SALES	2) Converting or organizing them into saleable products and services	various components of these
	3) Financing the sale of products and services on credit	activities

BUSINESS RISK

The overall business risk of an enterprise is the possibility that decision making about resources used in each phase of the cycle does not produce the intended financial results which would support or justify the continued use of resources for this economic activity. The financial results are shared to a greater or lesser degree by different financing sources of lenders and owners. The levels and conditions of lenders' and owners' participation reflect how the overall risk of the resource conversion is borne by the financing sources.

3
THE CONVERSION CYCLE

All enterprises acquire resources to be resold in the same or new form. Hopefully the sales price will provide enough money to cover the costs of producing and selling the output as well as maintaining the organizational support skills. The cost of the output has to include interest – the financial return to lenders. The residual between the sales price and total cost belongs to the owners, a reward for undertaking and being financially responsible for the activity.

Conversion activities are interrelated. The farmer converts seed to wheat. Many skills and resources go into the planting and harvesting activity. The farmer made many decisions about using land, labor, supplies, and tools. The farmer grew the wheat while bearing the risk of not recovering the costs of converting the seed to wheat (output) and selling it for more than the cost to produce it. When a flour mill acquires the wheat, value is added by converting it into flour, putting it into sacks and shipping it to buyers who resell the flour in small quantities to large numbers of users. The baker, a local purchaser of the flour, converts it along with other processed and raw resources, skills and equipment into baked goods which are sold to consumers and food stores. The latter buy the products and stack and display them along with other goods for purchase by the consumers. The food retailer bags the purchases, sometimes delivers them, and may even provide credit. Value added at the retail level is derived from using skills, buildings, and equipment associated with retail-selling activity.

Whether a small family store or a large supermarket, new products are acquired all the time, displayed on the shelves, and tested for their sales potential. The farmer too is usually investigating differ-ent kinds of seeds, fertilizers, equipment, and farming techniques which will hopefully improve production and quality. Each market is related to another. Each acquisition of resources and output by one entity is a sale of resources by another. Resources are acquired by business enterprises with the expectation of being sold. Many factors influence their cost and final conversion to cash. Are they saleable? At what price? When?

In general, the objective of each conversion activity undertaken by an individual or organization is to provide a new product or service to a different market, either facilitating a sale to another producer or to an end user/consumer. The overall risk of an economic enterprise buying and selling resources is two-fold: (1) the return of the financing invested in the transformation of resources will not take place or (2) the receipts realized from the sales will not cover the cost of what has been sold.

Some element of risk characterizes every transaction, business, and function of the conversion cycle. The risk is borne by the financiers, the owners and lenders to the activity, with the ultimate responsibility on the former.

Figure 3–1 translates the cycle of cash-to-resources-to-cash into the general functional areas of business risk common to most enterprises:

- Acquisition of resources involves risk of not getting the quality and quantity of the skills and materials needed.
- Production risk entails all the problems of organizing the transformation of skills and materials into finished products and services.

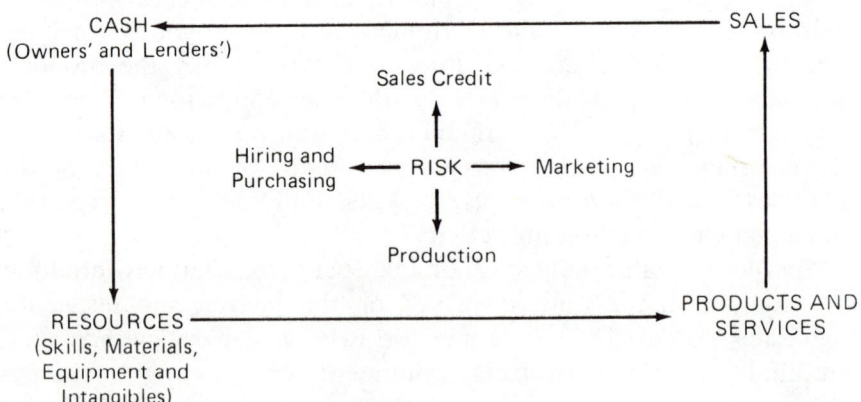

Figure 3–1.

- Marketing comprises all the efforts to make a product known and to complete its sales.
- Collection of cash from credit sales is the final risk in the cycle. Most businesses sell their goods and services on credit, thereby delaying the receipt of cash and creating the possibility, however slight, that they may not be paid.

Each enterprise in Figure 3–2 has a different cash-to-cash cycle and risk associated to a greater or less degree with one or more of the above functions. It also shows the interrelationship between the management functions within an enterprise and the financial and

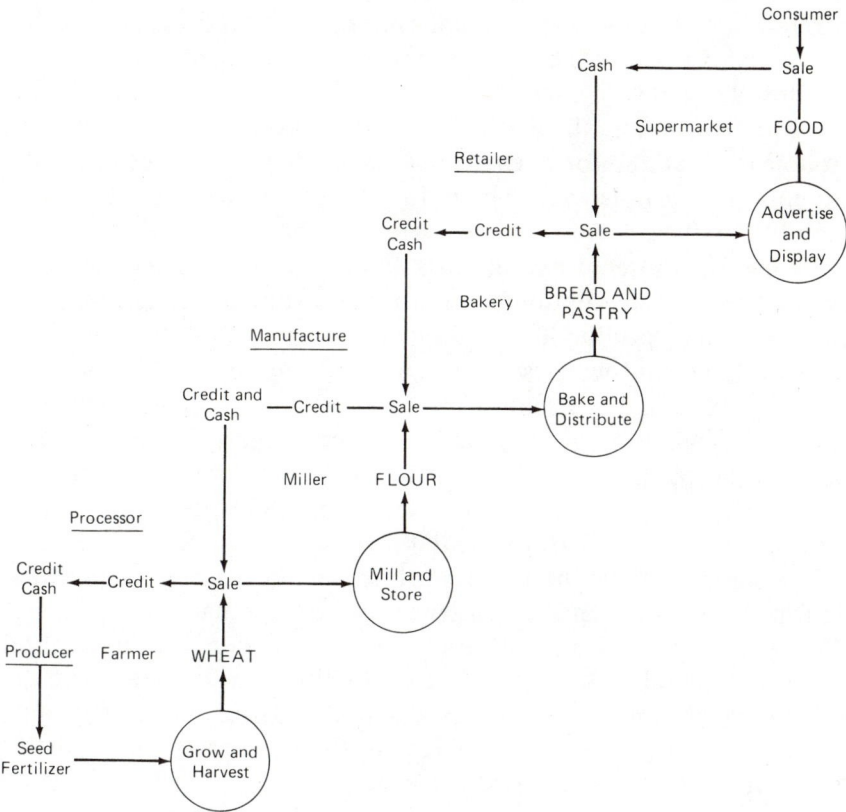

Figure 3–2.

resource markets. The particular configuration of resources and the financial structure and sources of an enterprise are reflected in the patterns of financial information about its operation.

HOW RESOURCE CONVERSION CYCLES DIFFER

Let's take a closer look at the resource conversion cycles of different business activities with which most of us are familiar.

Professional Services

Your dentist, after several years of training and working in different clinical settings, decides to start his or her own dental practice. With savings (owners' capital) and credit from suppliers and possibly a bank loan, a new office is set up with another dentist. They need to acquire the following resources for their dental business: office space and furniture which is rented and paid for on a monthly basis, modest decorations for a reasonably comfortable atmosphere for the patients and people working in the office, office equipment and supplies, postage, records books, a telephone, etc. The specialized skills involve those of the dentists (who may need some salary to live on) secretary/receptionist, and possibly a dental hygienist. The main pieces of "production" equipment are the dental chair complete with drill, air, and water sources, and an X-ray machine. These are very expensive and specialized pieces of equipment. They will most likely be useable for many years before needing replacement due to wear or obsolescence. The dentist also typically uses dental labs for various services as well as an accountant and other professionals for the normal activity of the dental practice.

The patient comes to the dentist for dental work. The dentist performs the work, and the patient is billed. The patient pays either all or part of the bill within 30 days or more depending on the total amount, the ability to pay, or other conditions of payment. If the patient has insurance that pays for dental services, the dentist must submit a formal bill with information to the third party for payment. Payment for services provided through this source could easily come three or four months after the services were performed. In the meantime, resources are being used and have to be replaced, i.e., skills. supplies, electricity, telephone, etc.

If you analyzed all the skills and materials required to produce dental services, you would find that when they are used up and the rate at which they are used up differs from when revenues are actually received for them. For example a receptionist takes calls and arranges appointments several weeks in advance. The cost of the services to produce and complete that appointment includes the skills of that receptionist as well as the dentist. Presumably the receptionist is paid weekly or bi-weekly to perform these skills. That pay period determines this cycle of conversion of skills for the end product or service. In effect, with each paycheck, labor in the form of different skills, is continuously bought, converted, and bought again. Most people are paid for their skills only as long as they perform according to some formal or informal agreement on what is being bought and sold, i.e., a job description. There is an implicit acceptance of the work performed as meeting these standards each time a paycheck is issued. In this sense, labor inputs are used up and acquired again, even though there may be formal contracts for a year's length of time.

Payment by the dentist for the office furniture may be within 30 days of its receipt, but this furniture will not be used up and need to be replaced for three years. The very expensive equipment will probably last seven to ten years. If credit from the seller is available, or a bank loan was used to acquire it, a string of payments will have to be made in the future. The cost of the use of these longer term resources will be recouped during their "useable life" by apportioning and including a periodic charge to the cost of producing the services. Thus, dental services mainly require the resource inputs of specialized dental and office skills and long-life, expensive equipment. Relatively few supplies and raw materials are necessary for producing the services. Thus, the timing of payment for resources used up diverges greatly from the income received from the generation (production) of the dental services. Other types of business activities have different compositions of timing of payments for the rest of those receipts from the sale of products and services which require them.

Retailing

If you look at your local supermarket, you will see that the main resource of the business is the food and household products available for purchase by the consumer. Fresh fruit and vegetables, processed foods, dairy products, meat, fish, poultry, and nonfood products fill the shelves. They can be classified as perishable and nonperishable; seasonal, prepacked, or bulk requiring weighing, cutting and wrapping; fast- or slow-moving; essential, "impluse" or "gourmet" items. Most of the sales activity in a supermarket is on a do-it-yourself basis. Display, not skilled salespeople, helps sell most of the products. Equipment requirements consist of standard refrigeration, lighting, shelving, scales, and cash registers. The latter two can be rented. Most of the skills required are not very specialized with the exception of those of the "buyers," especially of the perishable foods, and the accountant. Equipment maintenance is usually purchased when needed or under a service contract. Other labor includes stocking the shelves and counter help. With automatic scales, weighing and pricing is calculated electronically. The selling of most food to the consumer by the supermarket requires very little alteration from its original state. Most of it is prepared, or prepacked. Shoppers often select their own. The major economic function of a retailer is to attract customers and select and inventory products for their purchases. The economic role of this enterprise through which value is added is primarily an array of marketing and selling functions such as selection, storage, display, advertising, and customer services.

Most food stores rely on credit from their suppliers, whose terms of payment may be from a few days, or until the next delivery, a week or longer. Credit terms will at least be consistent with the perishability of the food items, the popularity of the produce (catsup, apple sauce, etc.), and most important the reputation of the store for paying its bills on time. Unlike the patients of the dentist, the stores' customers pay in cash as soon as they receive the products. Each day large amounts of products flow into and out of the store. Cash flows through the register and reordering of products is often done every day or two. The cash flow pattern differs greatly from the dentistry business. Most of the cost is composed of the wholesale cost of the items sold. Whereas most of the costs of the dental service are for the skilled labor required to produce it. The value added by the retailer to the original cost of the items sold is not a substantial proportion of the price because relatively low-cost skills and standard equipment are required to perform the retailing functions (marketing) of this type of retail sales. A gourmet food store would most likely require more costly organizational and selling skills, advertising resources, and services.

Other areas of consumer sales employ different marketing emphases and resources. Advertising for auto sales is primarily undertaken on a national basis, but local dealerships also participate in local advertising. Their resource requirements include their attractive showrooms, lively sales people and reliable service departments. Most have a stock of used cars. Many of the new products they sell are not available on the showroom floor. They are sold and ordered before delivery to customers. They do not finance the sales but assist in arranging car loans with financing institutions. Department stores on the other hand are large warehouses full of all kinds of products which are constantly purchased and sold. Advertising is a primary activity of their functioning. They manage the constant purchase and sale of goods to the consumers along with other functions such as delivery, gift wrapping, special promotions such as fashion shows, and often sales financing through credit card purchases.

There have been substantial effects from the credit card revolution on the retail enterprise. Consumers need not carry large amounts of cash or a checkbook. They can obtain immediate credit and are billed once a month. More important in terms of many retailers, it has eliminated the need to maintain consumer credit departments or make special arrangements for credit. The financing requirements of the retailer associated with providing consumer credit have been essentially eliminated. This shortened and strengthened the conversion cycle for the retailer. The credit card facility shifts the lending risk from the retailer to the credit card financier, a banking operation, except where large retailers such as Sears or Macy's offer their own credit facilities.

Manufacturing

In manufacturing activity, the conversion of resources occurs at a different pace from the way that the cash flows in and out of the enterprise. Value added to the raw materials depends on the complexity of the products. For example, in enterprises that build large engineered products such as airplanes, costly skills and equipment are the more important resources required to produce the saleable product. High quality materials for the airframe construction and engines are combined with expensive skills to produce the main structure. The final product also calls for many specialized components such as the radio and navigation instrumentation, electronic and hydraulic systems, which themselves require skilled labor and specialized manufacturing equipment. Other components such as seats, passenger lighting, interior finish, bathroom facilities, and food preparation equipment do not require a great amount of specialized resources for their manufacture. The time and amount of resources it takes to build a plane like the $30,000,000 Boeing 747 means that considerable dollars have to be spent on resources financed long before the plane will be sold.

The resource conversion cycle for the manufacture of such capital goods may in fact require several years. Hydroelectric power plants, large office buildings, chemical processing facilities, pipelines, railroads, etc., all require very lengthy construction periods involving a wide variety of skills, materials and machinery. Their costs are typically recouped over very long periods of time as economic benefits from their use are realized in the prices of the goods and services they produce.

Other manufacturing such as food processing may have much shorter production cycles. Raw food delivered at the processing factory where it is cleaned, cooked and packaged, or frozen and packaged is changed to a new product very rapidly. Most of the labor is unskilled and may often be needed only on a seasonal basis. The product may be stored in distribution warehouses either owned by the manufacturer or by an independent distributor whose function is to store and sell the products to the local retailers. The resources and financial cycle for the manufacturer involves the purchase and processing of the raw food and the sale of a finished product at a wholesale level. Where sales are made to independent distributors and retailers, credit is extended to the purchasers. It has varying length of time depending on industry conditions and competitions. The conversion cycle ends when the purchaser finally pays the bill.

Final sale of a product may also be part of the activities of a large "vertically-integrated" enterprise. Here the cycle would include different economic or market functions of manufacturing, warehousing/

distribution, wholesaling and direct selling through retail stores. Some food chains have their own food processing operations in addition to warehousing and distribution centers. Many clothing manufacturers have retail outlets where "seconds," excess inventory and even regular stock is sold to the public. The Levi Strauss Company, initially a jeans manufacturer, now has its own retail outlets. It sells to other retailers on a wholesale basis. Thus Levi's operations require both manufacturing and retail marketing resources. Their overall conversion cycle incorporates several related markets.

In sum, use of resources and their financing cycles depend on the complexity of the production activity and the extent to which other economic functions of storage, distribution, marketing and credit sales may be required or pursued as objectives of an enterprise. Financing the resources used by a given enterprise varies with differing lengths of economic functions of the conversion cycle and sales conditions.

Banking

A bank primarily functions as an intermediary between savers and borrowers. It does this by providing a safe depository for surplus cash for both consumers and commercial clients in the forms of savings accounts, checking accounts, and certificates of deposit. The cost of these funds is the interest paid out. A bank also borrows funds from other banks, the Federal Reserve system, commercial lenders, and long-term lenders. Owners provide ownership capital. The main output of a bank are the loans it makes to a variety of borrowers. Its revenues are primarily from interest on loans to clients. Thus banks are financial intermediaries; they manage the flow of surplus savings, temporary or longer term, to borrowers who in turn buy resources for conversion or who consume them. Banks also sell services such as management of personal investments (Trust Department), computerized payroll and billing services, international transfers of money, exchange of foreign currencies, and other services that facilitate the transfer of funds.

The flows of cash through a particular bank are influenced by the types of cycles the bank finances through its loan operations and the patterns of savings. Mortgage lending is relatively long-term, whereas construction lending is over a period of a couple of years. Consumer loans for cars range from two to four years. Where banks have a high proportion of commercial loans, the flow is influenced by the seasonality, strength, and characteristics of the economic activity, such as agriculture, manufacturing, military, tourist, or students. Savings patterns are influenced by ebb and flow of the local economy, family spending patterns and unemployment, as well as Easter and Christmas. They are also influenced by the competition of other organizations, the strongest of which in recent years has been the money market funds.

Through consumer credit card operations banks facilitate an immediate loan arrangement for consumer purchases in retail stores and restaurants thereby shortening the conversion cycle of the latter. They usually pay the retailer within two or three weeks of notification of the extension of credit to a consumer and then collect monthly payments from the credit card borrower.

There are many other sources of loans for commercial as well as consumer use. Insurance companies take in large amounts of insurance payments (premiums) that have to be constantly invested as well as paid out for accidents, medical care, retirement benefits, replacement of stolen articles, fire damage, etc. Insurance companies invest their money in commercial and consumer loans. The latter occur when policy holders borrow against their policies. Commercial mortgages on office buildings, large apartments and secured loans to business enterprises are typical income-generating investments for their funds. In this regard, they are similar to banks; however, considerable resources are used to market their products and services. Large sales forces are necessary to their operations.

To summarize, the conversion patterns of each enterprise emphasize different organizational functions and resource requirements depending on the economic functions they serve. The elements of overall risk of an enterprise are concentrated in the different functional areas accordingly. The financing requirements of an enterprise are mirrored in the types of resources utilized in the conversion and the length of time necessary to the cash flow cycle pertaining to their use. The financial risk of the conversion deals with the (1) recouping of the cost of resources and creditor financing used to make the sales and (2) rewarding the owners for the economic and financial risk they undertake in acquiring resources, converting, and selling the resulting output.

4

CONVERSION CYCLES AND ACCOUNTING MEASUREMENTS

Ongoing enterprises continually need resources in the conversion cycles. Resources are generally acquired and organized to produce goods and services in advance of sales. Each sale not only reduces the amount of resources available in the cycle, but also creates a partial recouping or freeing up of cash which returns to the financing source. (See Figure 4–1.) The sales price must incorporate or account for the amounts of physical resources and skills used directly and indirectly to make the sale. It also must include the costs of interest on lenders' financing, if resources are bought on credit. If the price does not include all these costs, the value of the output sold is less than the cost of resources used in the conversion. When sales value exceeds the cost, the cycle generates a surplus. Expanding business activity requires increased financing for additional resources in the cycle. Anticipated increases in sales promise to recoup the additional financial outlays for resources and reward the financing sources.

The financiers (lenders and owners) of an enterprise run the risk of the expected resource conversion faltering either because the output is unsaleable, the cost of the output is greater than the price buyers are willing to pay, or the framework of the future conversion cycle will be longer than originally projected. When sales do not generate the levels of cash anticipated at the time the resources were originally acquired, the owners' investment becomes subject to claims of the lenders (as defined in their loan agreements). Lenders' risks in the

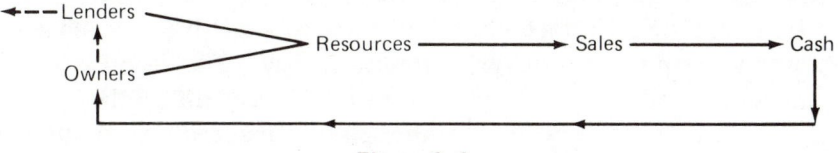

Figure 4–1.

conversion cycle are sheltered by the level of the owners' financial participation. The greater the owners' investment, the greater the security of the lenders' financial position and claims. In this context the owners' financing provides a backup to the lenders' position since it provides a cushion for the latter. For the owners – the greater their investment, the less the conversion cycle and cash generation are subject to obligations to lenders. A greater owners' investment reduces the risk of not meeting loan repayment obligations. In terms of costs, the less lenders' financing, the less the interest cost that needs to be recouped in the price of output sold.

Different types of businesses require different compositions of resources for their output as explored in Chapter 3. Resource conversion cycles vary among enterprises because of these compositions and the nature of the output and sales effort. The cash and credit requirements to start and maintain the conversion are as variable as the multiplicity of business activity. Depending on the use and availability of credit, the cash outlays and inflows will vary considerably in size and timing. The use of credit affects practically all economic activity. It partly finances the conversion cycle and it delays purchase payments, even though a transfer of ownership of goods and services – economic output – may have taken place.

CONVERSION: ECONOMIC AND FINANCIAL

A more detailed view of the conversion cycle concept recognizes distinct economic and financial elements: (1) the acquisition and transfer of resources through contracts of purchase and later sale, and (2) cash payments and receipts for the resources. The more efficient and productive the use of resources, the greater the output from and the shorter investment in the conversion cycle.

The cash conversion seldom synchronizes with the economic conversion. Credit offered by the seller is credit received by the buyer – a delay in payment for resources used in the buyer's conversion activities. In fact, the seller, through a credit sale, exchanges economic output for a buyer's promise to pay. The promise to pay is a separate and valuable resource, but one dependent on the buyer's generation of cash. Credit from the seller is financed directly by the owners or indirectly through the seller's use of other financing sources.

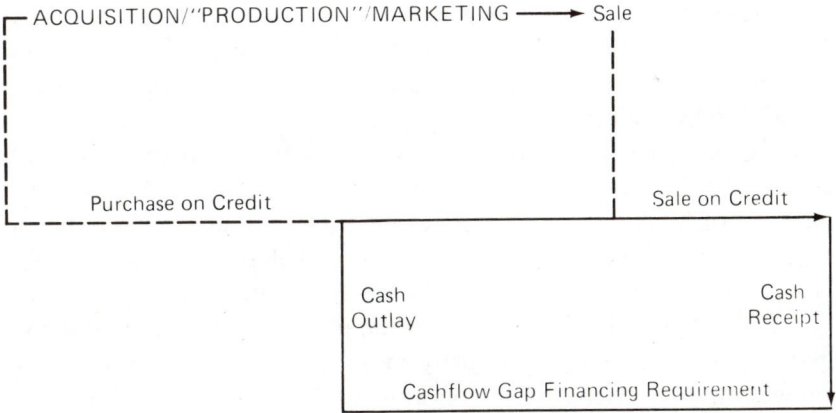

Figure 4–2.

Only when the buyer pays these obligations to the seller does the seller have use of the cash to repay creditors or to reinvest in the continuous activities of the conversion cycle. Ownership financing is constantly being reinvested in the cycle. The majority of enterprises also employ outside credit financing, either short- or long-term to carry resources through the cycle. Both fill the gap between the cash outflows and cash inflows, allowing for ongoing purchases of, and payments for, resources flowing through the conversion activities, as shown in Figure 4–2.

CASH FLOWS

Cash flow is financial terminology that refers only to the timing of patterns of cash payments and receipts of an entity.

Cash shortages occur as resources are purchased, products and services produced and sold. Besides owners' investment, borrowing allows for continuous operations with repayment expected from the future cash receipts. Borrowing takes on two dimensions: the short-term, for labor and materials or goods subsequently sold; and long-term, for resources that are used in production over long periods of time — primarily machinery, equipment, and buildings. Spending for these relatively expensive resources would cause a significant current cash flow deficit, without additional owners' financing or the use of borrowed funds. A long-term loan smooths the cash outflow over time, since repayments are made during the productive life of the resources employed.

In the everday world of business management in our economy, certain conditions and specific decisions influence the aggregate patterns of cash flows and therefore influence changes in the net cash flow levels of an entity. These are seasonal, such as in agricultural-based business; and cyclical, such as the manufacturing of heavy machinery. In addition, industry trade practices often determine the credit terms of sales. A company may or may not control the time framework for paying wages because of trade practice, union contracts, or other factors. The pay period can be daily, weekly, biweekly, or monthly. Bonuses, commissions, and royalty payments vary for different resources and by practices of different companies. Social Security taxes have to be paid at least quarterly, and with large companies on a weekly basis. Business income taxes are due four times a year according to state and federal laws. Insurance payments and other contracted obligations also influence the patterns of payments. Repayment schedules of term loans for equipment and buildings may be composed of many or few commitments over the length of the loan. They could be quarterly payments during the full term of the loan, be it 3, 10, or 25 years, or a one-time payment at the end of the loan period.

The opposite effect of a series of payments leveling a cash outflow takes place when a company sells an unused manufacturing or warehouse facility. The one-time sale of such a major resource provides a sudden inflow of cash. The same is true when new ownership shares or long-term debts (bonds) are sold.

While credit is commonly used to make sales, discounts for early payment are also part of many sales agreements. Customers who take discounts pay less to meet their obligations. Their early payment positively influences the timing of the inflows of cash to the seller, but reduces the value of the receipts. Since the seller has to finance credit sales either with the owners' financing, or through bank borrowing, it's often worthwhile offering the buyer a discount for early payment. Early payment reduces the conversion cycle time. The cash available can be used to reduce debt, thus reducing the interest cost, or it can be reinvested in the cycle to earn additional profits. Some businesses sell C.O.D. (cash on delivery), and others require the purchaser to make a deposit in advance of production and delivery. A magazine subscription involves a receipt of the full price of one or more years of future output, often well in advance of much of the resource acquisition!

The same transaction — the sale or transfer of ownership of resources — influences opposing decisions involved in the individual cash flows of the buyer and the seller. For any business, insofar as payments for resources can be legitimately delayed, and debt from sales on credit speedily collected, the cash flow gaps are shortened.

The management of credit from and for sales is often a significant part of the operating strategies of businesses. For example, large consumer goods manufacturers like Gillette and Polaroid typically provide generous credit terms for their sales. By doing so, they finance the distribution function of independent wholesalers who store, sell, and provide credit to local retailers. The conversion cycle of these manufacturers covers a lengthy period largely because of extended financial support of the marketing function carried out by their customers.

Quite the opposite happened to fashion clothing manufacturers during 1982. Interest rates were rising rapidly, and retail sales were slowing down. Many of these manufacturers found their customers increasingly late in paying their bills, much later than the due dates. The retailers financed their activities with terms of credit involuntarily extended from the manufacturers. How could the retailers get away with voiding their obligations? They simply said that if you want to sell to us during these hard times, we'll set the payment terms. Small manufacturers in this highly competitive environment had little choice. They paid their banks high rates of interest to finance the longer-than-normal credit terms extracted by their large customers. In effect, the retailers borrowed from the manufacturers who borrowed from their banks in anticipation of future payments from their customers.

Cash flows for an entity are a continuously changing combination of short- and long-term flows reflecting the particular aggregation of resources in use at a given time. The structure of their financing — the types and amount of credit and owners' investment — reflects the varying patterns of expected cash flows from the sale or consumption of individual resources and the risks of economic and financial conversion.

The art of managing the finances of an enterprise deals with reducing the risk of not being able to finance cash flow gaps and minimizing the cost of doing so.

Cash Flow Projections

Most company managers figure out the financial flows of their operations in order to determine the need for short-term commercial financing and their financial ability to repay long-term debt obligations.

Resource conversion patterns and cash collection experience indicate the time framework for future payments and receipts. Sales made on credit during one month may be collected in the following months. Suppliers offering credit for materials or products used in production will have to be paid according to their credit terms. The volume of output to be produced during any particular period of time will require the financing of certain resource use. The volume of expected sales will produce future cash inflows. Just look at sales versus the cash inflow patterns in Figure 4–3.

Total expected receipts from economic conversion would also consider any one-time sale of used equipment or buildings. In addition, new cash investment from owners and lenders increases (momentarily) the total cash receipts flow. If all sales had been on a cash basis, then cash receipts would equal sales in the same month. However, the economic conversion and the financial conversion are quite separate. The breakdown of expected cash receipts into a time schedule is based on the experience of an enterprise in offering credit and managing the collection activity. A change in credit policy or the attention given to making sure that customers pay their bills will result in a very different cash inflow pattern with the same level of sales.

The same disparity exists between the acquisition of resources and the flow of payments for them. Here the consideration would be based on projected monthly production to meet sales plans. The amounts of labor and materials acquired would be determined by the

	Actual		Projected					
Month	Feb	March	April	May	June	July	Aug	Sept
Sales	300	200	100	100	200	300	400	400
(Economic Conversion)								
Cash Receipts								
1-30 days (20%)	60	40	20	20	40	60	80	80
31-60 days (50%)	150	150	100	50	50	100	150	200
61-90 days (30%)	120	90	90	60	30	30	60	90
Total	330	280	210	130	120	190	290	370
Receipts from Sales								

Financial Conversion (vertical label at left)

Figure 4–3.

expected levels of output and the complexity of the conversion activities, i.e., manufacturing, wholesaling, or retailing. While labor would most likely be paid concurrently with its use, payment for materials is often subject to the terms of credit offered by the suppliers. Most of the organizational costs would occur on a regular basis. Marketing efforts might vary somewhat from month to month depending on the seasonal nature of the business or new product introductions. The sales projection in Figure 4–3 reflects a seasonal (fall-winter) business. Thus, advertising expenditures might be greater during the middle of the year than during the early months. Here, too, credit arrangement would influence cash payments. As mentioned earlier, there might be specific times of the year when particular payments are due, such as taxes, insurance, loan repayments. Since businesses often buy new equipment, these important one-time

TABLE 4-1.

	ACTUAL		PROJECTED					
MONTH	FEB.	MARCH	APRIL	MAY	JUNE	JULY	AUG.	SEPT.
Production (1,000 units @ $5.00/unit	15	10	20	25	30	30	40	40
($1,000)								
Labor ($3.00/unit)	45	30	60	75	90	90	120	120
Materials ($2.00/unit; 30 days credit)	40	30	20	40	50	60	60	80
Managerial	85	85	90	90	90	95	95	90
Advertising	20	10	30	40	40	30	20	20
Machinery	15			60				
Other: Taxes			40			20		
Total Cash Payments	205	155	240	305	270	275	295	310

purchases will either cause an immediate increase in cash payments if credit is not used, or a future increase in periodic cash outflows will occur depending on the conditions of repayment of a loan agreement. While cash inflow derives mainly from a sales pattern, cash outflow derives from the scheduling of production and the credit arrangements from suppliers.

Assume the production information in Table 4–1 was prepared for the forementioned sales projections.

Any variation on the particular pattern of individual resource payments will change the cash outflow. Thus, if the company was able to purchase materials on a credit sale of 60 days, cash payments would shift further ahead of production and closer to the cash receipts from sales. Any delay in paying for the machinery, or planning purchases and utilization at different times, would also change the cash outflow patterns. Matching the cash inflow with the cash outflow defines the expected cash gap that must be financed:

	FEB.	MARCH	APRIL	MAY	JUNE	JULY	AUG.	SEPT.
Receipts	330	280	210	110	120	190	290	370
Payments	(205)	(155)	(240)	(305)	(270)	(275)	(295)	(310)
Net Cash Flow	125	125	(30)	(195)	(150)	(85)	(5)	60

Continued high-level sales in the period of October through January would generate additional surplus cash to be used to repay borrowed funds that may have financed continuing operations in the April through August period. If the $60,000 machinery purchase in May was partly financed with a $50,000 loan payable in equal installments every three months over two-and-one-half years (ten payments of principal plus interest), then the net deficit for May would be reduced by $50,000, and August's deficit would increase by the amount of the loan repayment. The cash outflow for this particular resource would be smoothed out over time and matched with cash inflows from expected sales of the resources over time.

In sum, the cash flow patterns result from many decisions about the acquisition, timing, and the use of resources; credit terms and policies of buyers and sellers; and the use of financing (debt) to support conversion activities. At any given time framework of a conversion cycle, the flows of cash, both in and out of an enterprise, vary, resulting in net surpluses and shortages. The surpluses or shortages may last for a period of weeks, months, or even years. If receipts from sales of output are reasonably predictable, commercial loans and other debt financing are made with the expectations and the projections that cash shortages will become surpluses. Such cash flow shortages do not mean that sales are unprofitable; only that cash outlay for resources and cash inflow from sales occur at differing points of the conversion cycle.

Analysis of the timing of cash coming in and going out of an enterprise reveals a multitude of decisions about resource acquisition and use and credit availabilities. However, it does not provide a calculation of costs of producing a specific sale or amount of sales. Resources that are purchased at a given point of time are converted at differing rates of time subsequent to their acquisition.

COSTS OF SALES

As we have seen in the earlier examples, some resources can be converted almost immediately while others are converted or used up over long periods of time. The price of the final products or services realized in a sale must cover these costs of resources partly or fully used up in producing the output in order for the cycle to continue. For example, the refrigeration equipment and the shelving in the supermarket are used up over several years, whereas the actual items on and in them may be sold quite rapidly within a few days after they are delivered to the store by the supplier. This equipment used by the supermarket is necessary to the business activity of selling food to consumers. To include the total cost of this equipment resource in only one year of sales would sharply increase the cost of producing the final output, and therefore the price. And more important, it would mean that these resources were used up to produce the sale. In fact that would not be true. The equipment is usable in the cycle for many years. However, some portion of the original expenditure, the acquisition cost, must be included in the price received for the products sold. The cash inflows from sales are recoupments of component costs of resources used to produce the sale.

Accounting for the costs of output sold at any given time involves the problem of allocating a dollar value to the amounts of resources used up in different activities of the conversion cycle and the costs of financing it. Economic costs (cost of production) change not only with the suppliers' prices but also with the particular mix of resources used. Automation may reduce total costs of the final product, and it will definitely change the composition of the costs. Less labor costs per unit would be required. New methods of production, new products, and new organizational functions of greater emphasis on certain activities, i.e., a major advertising campaign, means changing valuations of the amounts of resource components used in a particular level of the output. Determining how much of the resources is consumed in the production and sale of the product or service involves abstracting and categorizing information from a multitude of conversion transactions.

Financing costs and interest charges on borrowed money vary with the rates charged by the lenders as well as with the amount of borrowed funds utilized by owners to finance the conversion cycle. Whenever a high level of the total financing of resources in a conversion cycle lies with creditors, interest costs as a portion of the price charged for the resource used and sold will be relatively high in relation to other costs.

Accounting For A Sale

Consider just the sale of a specific item in the local supermarket. The milk in the store refrigerator is purchased every couple of days. It is sold to the consumer, and the dairy is paid regularly. The refrigerator provides the cooling to prevent it from spoiling. Some tiny portion of the cost of the refrigerator has to be included in the price of every container sold. While the wholesale cost of the container of milk (the price paid to the dairy by the supermarket) is recouped in every sale, only a tiny part of the refrigeration equipment cost is recouped. The credit from the dairy for the milk is very short term, since the product is ready to be used and has to be sold in a short period of time. Financing for the refrigeration is long term, either provided by commercial lenders, owners themselves, or most commonly by a combination of the two.

The language and perspective of finance and accounting sees all business activity in terms of varying resource conversion cycles divided into two major accounting categories: short term, less than one year; and long term, greater than one year.

Product or service costs are associated with either short-life, or long-life resources utilization. Thus, the price of a quart of milk to the consumer is composed of the following:

(acquisition)   wholesale price from the dairy

plus

(conversion)   *a portion of:*
                      the wages and salaries of the workers and
                          managers in the store
                      advertising
                      insurance
                      bookkeeping and accounting

the maintenance cost of and electricity for
the refrigeration equipment
rent for space
the annual using up or wearing down of
the refrigeration equipment, the lighting
system, the cash registers, and shopping
carts

plus

(credit financing)   the interest on the borrowed money used
(1) to buy the milk (if applicable); and
(2) to finance the refrigeration equipment
and other long-life resources

plus

(owner's reward)   surplus between price and cost, for taking the
business risk

If the space was owned and not rented, then some portion of the
value of the building would have to be charged for its annual use.

In contrast, in the operations of a power company, a kilowatt of
electricity has its particular configuration of costs. A large portion
of the costs relates to the generating equipment and power distribution system. Since these long-life resources are usually financed
with substantial amounts of borrowed funds, interest costs are also a
major component of the total cost to produce a unit of power. A
dental services business would show a substantial portion of its
costs paid out for skills and services of professionals involved.

In sum, each of the cost components can be related to the resource
transactions in the conversion cycle. The *profit and loss statements*
(sales/cost reports) mirror the different combinations of resources
used and financing structures. (See Figure 4–4.)

To determine surplus or loss from a sales or group of sales during
a time period, measurements have to be made of the dollar values of
the portions of resources used to produce the sales. Accounting
methodologies are designed to abstract those values from the flow of
resources into an ongoing conversion activity.

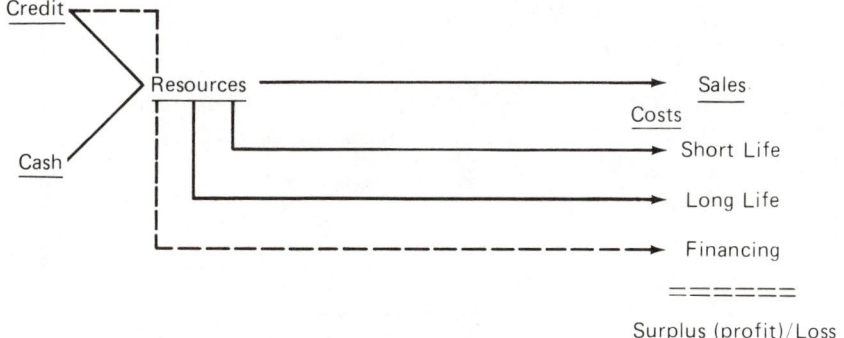

Figure 4–4.

AVAILABLE RESOURCES AND THEIR FINANCING

If the conversion activities of an enterprise were momentarily stopped, unused resources would be available. Either those resources would have been fully paid for, or creditors would be owed. Payments to creditors may be due the next day or many years into the future. They may or may not coincide closely with the specific conversions of the resources to cash. While loan repayments usually have a clear pattern of due dates in the future, the estimation of costs of resources used up from a constant and changing supply of available resources is subject to interpretation. Revenue values are determined by a sales agreement between buyer and seller about the value of output transferred. The cost (value) of resources used up to make sales is abstracted and deducted from the original purchase prices paid for resources acquired. The difference — the value of unused resources — will be available for future conversion.

The methods of accounting for costs of resources used to produce a given portion of sales depends on differing accounting methods and political (tax policy) rationales for determining the value of the amounts óf resources used up, both short- and long-life, to produce a sale. The accounting measurements that serve for determining costs of sales also serve for determining the remaining value of unsold resources.

Sales and purchases constantly change the level of resources in, and financing of, the conversion cycle of an enterprise. Available

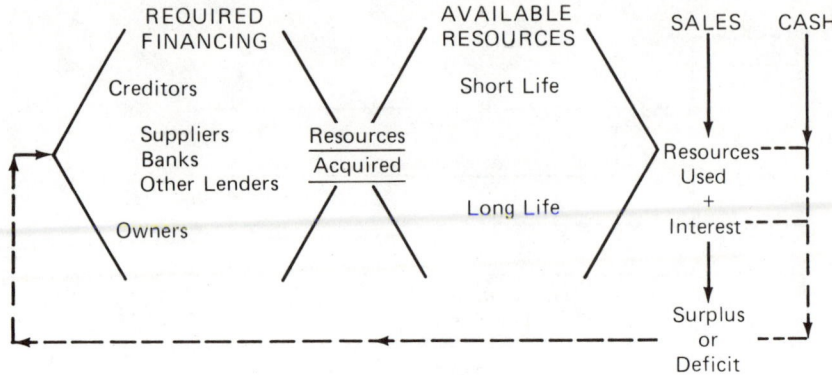

Figure 4–5.

resources and debts to creditors are constantly changing as shown in Figure 4–5.

A sale involves a transfer of ownership, a reduction of resources, and the generation of cash. For financing sources it reduces the risk of conversion. Acquiring resources adds to their risk. The accounting measurements that determine the costs of sales also determine the remaining value of unsold resources. A status report of resources available, and debt owned, can be determined at any time. Two such reports that frame a sale or group of sales show the changes in the conversion status, i.e., the many elements of economic and financial risk of conversion. This status report is a *balance sheet*, the name derived from the idea that the value of each resource purchase equals the amount of financing. The conversion value of the output is unknown until it is sold.

Part II
The Accountant's Interpretation of the Use of Resources

5
ABOUT ACCOUNTING MEASUREMENTS AND ACCOUNTING PRINCIPLES

The collecting, organizing, verifying and presenting of financial information about the many transactions that compose the business functions in the conversion cycle are the main subjects of accounting. Whether an enterprise is small or large, the keeping of elementary financial records, the "books," is necessary in order to "account for" the financial effects of business decisions that were made in the past. Financial reports drawn from this information are historical in content. Their formats specifically aim at measuring the costs and revenues associated with past decisions, changes in the composition and amounts of resources, and changes in the financing of the cycles of their use.

Business decision making involves using the available skills and material resources or aquiring them for a continued economic activity, and channeling or managing the financing of these resources. The financial information (if relevant, timely, and reliable) helps guide future decisions about the use and availability of resources and financing strategy. For example, the decision to expand production and marketing of a product line starts with calculations about potential sales (marketing) and profitability (production). It also requires various additional nonfinancial and financial information which includes marketing strategy, the assessment of current use of available resources (skills and production facilities), expected resource requirements, and a translation of costs of those resources. A financial plan reflects an expected pattern of resource utilization and costs. By estimating future sales, a cash flow can be projected which shows expected total financing requirements over time.

The complexity of keeping track of the information is not just a matter of the size of the business operations. Each industry, indeed each entity, reflects an emphasis on different components of the resource conversion functions and the financing of them. The organization of the financial information collection procedures (bookkeeping) and the financial controls (financial management) reflects not only the financial flow characteristics of each enterprise, but also the organized and fairly standardized recording and reporting formats of the accounting profession. Accounting terminology describes and categorizes, in monetary terms, the different transactions in the resource conversion cycles. It is the universal language of business and finance. These accounting formats facilitate communication of relatively uniform data compilations to various decision makers/investors, creditors, managers, and government authorities.

According to the American Accounting Association, the theory of accounting consists of "a set of basic concepts and assumptions and related principles that explain and guide the accountant's action in identifying, measuring and communicating economic activity."[1] Though the theory may be stated as such, in fact the profession is continually redefining the essential assumptions, principles, and concepts. Thus far, the profession has developed "generally accepted accounting principles (GAAP)" that practitioners use for professional guidance in carrying out their work. The principles provide not only a unifying standard for the profession, but they also allow users to assume conformity to certain accounting standards. These principles are a product of considerable deliberation and debate organized by the Financial Accounting Standards Board (FASB) whose function is to focus on accounting issues. This board has wrestled with the questions of the objectives of financial reporting and has stated some preliminary findings in an exposure draft entitled "Objectives of Financial Reporting by Business Enterprises," 1979.

Their statement primarily says that financial reporting should provide useful information to present and potential investors (both owners and creditors) and others to aid them in making rational decisions. The information should be understandable to those who have a reasonable knowledge of business and economic activity. It should help investors and other users assess the "amount, timing and uncertainty" of their cash flow claims as well as the cash flow of the enterprise. It should also provide information about and changes in

---

[1] "A Statement of Basic Accounting Theory," *American Accounting Association*. Sarasota, 1966.

the resource levels and claims to those resources. These objectives signal a constant vigilance about the qualitative nature of information, a serious and fundamental responsibility of the profession. That information be relevant, reliable and timely, circumscribes the accounting function in service of the user. These qualities aid the user's predictions of the outcomes of possible decisions affecting the resource conversion cycle. But, accounting is not a predictive function. Accountants are not decision makers; that is the territory of people they serve — the owners, the creditors, and the managers.

UNDERLYING ASSUMPTIONS

As a practical matter, accounting professionals have some common starting points which are necessary to carry out their work:

1. *Economic Entity.* Accounting information pertains to a unit or activity which is treated as an entity. The entity is viewed as having a life separate from its owners, employees, or others. The entity is not required to be a legal corporation. It need only be an economic entity in terms of its use of resources and financial obligations.
2. *Going Concern.* The assumption here is that the entity is viewed as having a continuing life unless there is existing evidence to the contrary. Its resources are expected to be constantly used and replaced in a conversion cycle.
3. *Monetary Measurement.* Financial statements are expressed in money measurements. The dollar is the unit of measurement in the United States. This measurement assumes a "stable" value; consequently, information is expressed on a historical basis, not in terms of purchasing power of the unit of currency.
4. *Periodic Reporting.* Because of the assumption of continuing life of an entity, financial information in order to be useful to owners and creditors needs to report activities on a continuing basis. Periodic reporting that is comparable and continuous characterizes the basis of the usefulness to the concerned parties.

5. *Estimation and Judgment.* Because financial reporting is on a periodic basis (if for no other reason than for annual reporting of income taxes) sometimes estimates are required about the risks of conversion of various resource elements in the cycle. For example, accountants have to make some determination of how much sales on credit will ultimately turn into uncollectable debts of customers.

Accountants are always concerned about the realizeable valuation of resources used in the conversion cycle since their perspective deals with an ongoing business. They must express their professional opinions about the future economic viability of an entity when the continuation of a conversion cycle may be in doubt. This type of situation arises when the possible negative consequences of a major legal action might put a company out of business. It also occurs when loan payments coming due cannot be met.

THE PROBLEM OF VALUE OF RESOURCES

Accounting deals with the subject of *value* by using prices paid and received at the time of exchange of resources between buyer and seller. When there is overwhelming evidence that the current exchange value of a resource is substantially different from its historical value, then an adjustment is made. For example, when products prove to be unsaleable in the marketplace, their value based on the cost of resources used to make them has to be adjusted for scrap value. However, the adjustment requirement primarily applies to values of resources that have fallen during the conversion cycle. A piece of land owned for many years, for example, is valued at its acquisition price, even though it may be saleable at a much higher price.

While historical cost is the guiding measurement perspective, modifications are made based on (1) current replacement cost, (2) current value expected to be gained from an unhurried sale of resources, (3) expected or *net realizeable* value in the normal course of a business, and (4) revaluation based on the effects of inflation. The valuation adjustments have been developing as a result of the accounting profession's concern with the relevancy of the financial information. The topic of historical valuation is particularly sensitive at times of high levels of inflation as experienced in the early and late 1970's and early 1980's.

MATCHING COSTS AND BENEFITS

As discussed and presented graphically in earlier chapters, expenditures for resources generally precede the sales of output. Consequently, determining the differential between price received in a sale and paid out to produce the item sold requires a matching of prior costs with related output sold. From the accountant's perspective, the ideal is to relate costs of output to the sales values. The most fundamental aspect of accounting is reflected in the choice of reporting bases. If financial reports were compiled on a *cash (flow) basis*, purchases and sales would be recorded only when payments were made and receipts deposited. For the most part, they would be unrelated to one another, especially when expensive long-life resources were necessary to produce output.

Consequently, cash flow reporting would not accurately portray changes in the levels of resources in use and changing financial obligations supporting them in the conversion cycle. Ultimately, purchases and sales have to match in order to determine the economic viability of that cycle. The timely calculation of costs of the sales gives an immediate measure of the viability of the conversion cycle — a need for managers, creditors, and owners.

Accrual-based reporting is the method of reporting revenues and expenses in relation to transactions involving resource exchanges, rather than actual cash payments or receipts. It reflects availability of resources and changing financing obligations. This reporting approach provides a more accurate base for planning and decision making affecting the continuous operation of the conversion activities. The changes in what an entity owns or uses and owes provide the data for decisions about the financing of the conversion cycle. Allocation and abstraction of costs from past resource expenditures provide information about the profitability of a conversion cycle.

AN OVERVIEW OF THE ACCOUNTANTS' TRANSLATIONS

At any given time in the conversion cycle, resources will be available for future use and sale. Their acquisition value will not only be allocated to future costs of sales, but in the records of a business they will also correspond to an equivalent amount of required financing. Purchases are made with credit, owners' funds, or both. Purchase value equals financing at the time of acquisition. Sales made subsequent to that point in time will reduce the level of available resources. However, with ongoing activity, additional resources will most likely be acquired for future production and sales. Consequently, the levels of resources available for the conversion activities will change every day in a continuing cycle. So too, will the levels of financing. Thus, at the beginning and ending of a sales period (a segement of a conversion cycle) a different composition of financing will reflect changes in the levels of resources in use and their financing sources.

Surplus from sales — the difference between cost and price received — belongs to the owners. It can be reinvested in the conversion cycle or withdrawn as distributions to the owners under the title of *dividends*. Such distributions are separate from salaries which may be paid to owners who provide skills, except in single-owner businesses (sole proprietorships) or professional partnerships such as law firms where earnings from the business activity constitute the salaries. Salaries, as costs of resources, flow out of an enterprise. Surplus of a particular sales period, if not paid out to owners, becomes additional owners' financing of the conversion cycle. Losses are a reduction of the owners' investment. They signify that the value received from sales was less than the costs of the resources and financing used to produce the sales. The lost value is reflected in a reduction of the owners' investment, because creditors are paid based on their loan agreements.

Accountants measure the conversion activities on a periodic basis. They calculate the profit or loss from sales and changes in the levels of resources and financing mix. They prepare financial information about past conversion transactions in a sequential framework as shown in Figure 5–1.

This perspective translates into three major accounting reports:
- *Income Statement (Profit and Loss)*. What was the value of the resources used to produce the sales and financing costs of a given time period? Was it greater or less than the value received?

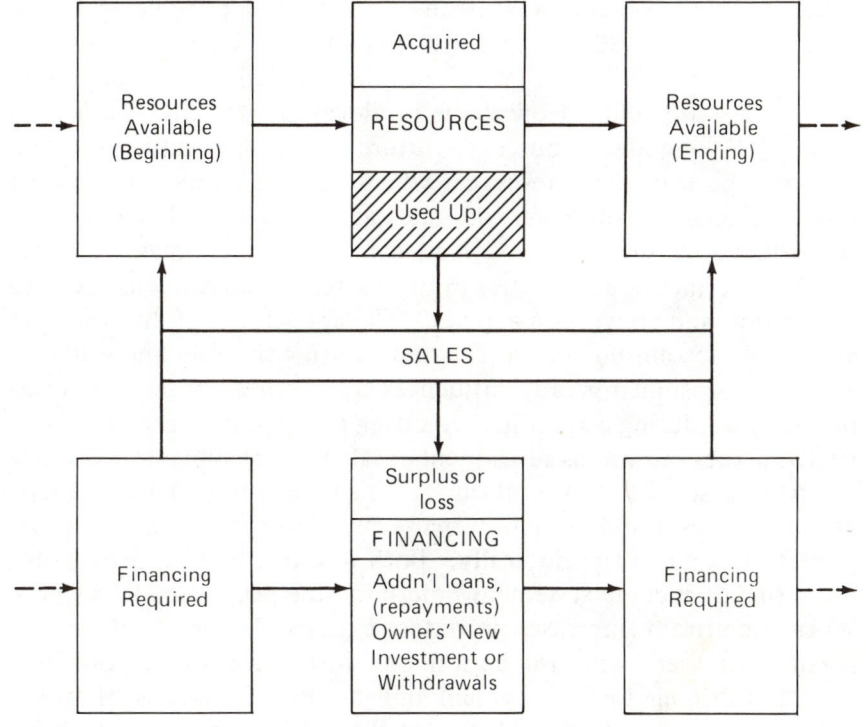

Figure 5–1.

- *Balance Sheet.* At a given time (beginning or end of a sales period) what resources were available for future conversion and sale? How were they financed?
- *Changes in the Financial Condition (Source and Use of Funds)* What net changes in the flow of owners' and creditors' sources from operations or outside funding accounted for the net changes in the levels of resources available for future conversion?

INTERCONNECTION OF FINANCIAL REPORTS

From Figure 4–6 one can see that the value of resources used in sales is both a cost on the income statement, and a reduction of the available resources on the balance sheet.   The accounting (and management) problems arise from the different possible methods, or rationales, for allocating a portion of the acquisition costs of available resources to units of output sold and to the period in which they are sold. How do you allocate part of the acquisition cost of a long-life resource to future conversion activity? And suppose the short-lived resources which you are selling daily have a rapidly changing acquisition cost, such as crude oil in 1979 and 1980. How do you value what you have sold and what remains unsold? What is the measure of surplus in the context of continuous resource acquisition and conversion activity? The application of different and acceptable accounting techniques to measuring the sales and values of resources consumed greatly influences the reported or measured surplus (or loss) during a specific accounting period. Each technique is reflected in the continuous adjustment of valuation of available resources.

Changes in the composition of financing often have dramatic effects on costs and cash flow patterns. More credit means more interest is paid out periodically. Both resource costs and financing costs on the income statement determine the generation of surplus. When significant increases in interest costs do occur, it usually means that there will also be a major shift in future cash outflows due to fulfilling loan repayment obligations. Schedules of future payments are usually provided with the balance sheet which shows the changes in the loan categories and levels of credit financing. Actual changes in the financing levels during an accounting period are reflected in the statement of changes in the financial condition.

VALUE MEASUREMENTS AND CASH FLOW

The measurement of the cost and surpluses of related sales does not answer the question of whether financing sources and terms facilitate the continuity of the conversion cycle. Though a business may produce a surplus in any given accounting period, it still must be able to pay its bills during that period. A bill, or loan payment, often includes payment for resources that will be sold in the future. Furthermore, except for retail businesses that deal in cash, sales do not equal cash revenues. Most sales in the economy involve exchanges of resources for customers' promises to pay in the future, thus delaying cash receipts.

Ability to pay obligations due in the future reflects the cash flow consequences of past transactions as well as those of future sales. The balance sheet indicates the types and terms of financing of the resources available for future conversion. It indicates both the future cash outflow obligations arising from past resource purchases and financing agreements and the cash inflow potential of *past*, uncollected sales made on credit. While past sales may be some indicator of future resource conversion, it cannot in fact be known if or when the sale of resources on hand will occur, or if the sales value will recoup the expenditures incurred in the past.

The accounting task is rarely one of guessing the future. The future risk of the conversion cycle is largely unknown. For example, the financial reports of Braniff Airlines reflected the company's expansion decisions in their purchase of a large fleet of airplanes. They also showed the extensive increase in the level of long-term credit obligations which financed these resources. Past sales had been expanding rapidly. The future looked promising! No one had expected a future of major fuel cost increases, declining economy, and fare wars which all reduced the cash inflow relative to the expanded outflow required by the loan repayments. Eventually, the company was unable to meet its obligations and ceased operations.

PROFIT AND NOT-FOR-PROFIT BUSINESS ACTIVITY

Though this book is oriented to the profit-making enterprise, the same accounting concerns and financial principles are involved in cooperative enterprises where owners/members share the benefits, as well as the risks, of the conversion activity. The economic benefit, which is primarily the distribution of the expected surplus from costs and revenues, may be passed on directly to the owners/members in the form of lower prices to members as purchasers of the output (retail food co-op), or higher revenues to members as sellers of products to the entity (cooperative dairy). The essential aspects of economic and financial viability of the conversion cycle remain the same: (1) the cost to produce must equal the revenues received and (2) financing must be structured to facilitate or support the conversion time of the resources involved. There is no difference in the nature of the profit or nonprofit conversion cycle, nor in the accounting of the cost-revenue equation. The only variation occurs in the way that the net benefits, the surplus, is shared. Generation of surpluses between resource exchanges still motivates the owners/members who undertake the economic activity, invest their funds, and obligate the entity when loans are used.

6
IS THE BUSINESS PROFITABLE?

THE PROFIT AND LOSS FOCUS

The price, the value received in the conversion of resources, will determine whether the value of the resources used for the output sold will be returned to the conversion cycle, in effect becoming the funding source. The income statement focuses on accounting for these values. It measures only the recouping of the costs of the resources sold; thus, a surplus or deficit has been generated. This calculation does not refer to cash flows since resources may have been purchased long before they are used, and cash revenues may arrive long after a transfer (sale) of resources takes place. The measure and risk of timing of the cashflows are separate. Consequently, a company can show a surplus, but be unable to pay its bills!

People who operate businesses deal directly with continuous flows of payments and receipts transactions. Periodic measures of profits, or losses, are abstracted from these transactions. Resources that were used up in the creation of each sale have to be measured to determine the costs of the particular part of the conversion cycle. Those measurements of costs are at any one time portions of continuous flows of resources in the overall cycle. Each resource is consumed at a different rate over time. In addition, costs of credit which finances the resources owned by an enterprise must be included in the total cost of a sale.

ABSTRACTING AND RELATING COSTS

The framework of accounting for sales transactions covers at most, a period of one year — the standard taxation period. Record keeping is usually done on a daily basis, showing all the individual transactions of acquisition and sales, payments and receipts. It is important to note again that cost determinations are on an accrual basis. They are abstracted from when they were incurred, or obligated, rather than when they were paid. They are matched to (1) the product sold, and (2) the time periods. Sales revenues are recognized at the point in time when resources are exchanged.

Matching of costs to sales is determined on two bases: (1) the resource costs directly incurred to make the product, as in manufacturing or buying the merchandise for a retail business; (2) other costs that are necessary to the ongoing business activities, such as administration, advertising, personnel training, research, accounting, and interest on borrowed funds, but do not relate directly to specific sales. These expenses are matched to sales transactions by *periodic* measurement. So any given period of sales will usually show two sets of expenses — those directly related to products or services sold, and those indirect expenses of administration, marketing, technical expertise, and financing of the conversion cycle.

A sale is recorded at a point in time when an exchange of ownership of goods, or benefit of services, takes place; not when payment is received. Thus, a sale on credit delays payment, but is generally recognized as revenue when the economic benefit of resources is transferred to a buyer.

CATEGORIZATION OF COSTS

In the sale of a unit of milk in the supermarket example in the previous chapter, various and diverse resource costs compose the *price*. They include:

- *Cost of the milk* (wholesale price paid to the dairy)
- *Wages and salaries or payroll* (cashiers, food buyer, bookkeeper, store manager, and other store personnel)
- *Payroll and social security taxes* (related to personnel costs)
- *Supplies* (paper bags, cleaning, price tags)
- *Advertising* (signs, flyers, newspapers)
- *Rent* (space)
- *Improvements* (lighting and other fixtures, shelving, painting)
- *Equipment* (refrigeration, cash registers, carts, air conditioning)

- *Business taxes and licenses* (right to operate)
- *Services* (garbage disposal, telephones, maintenance, accounting, legal)
- *Insurance* (for customers, fire/flood, and robbery)
- *Shrinkage* (spoilage, damage, theft)
- *Interest* (cost of borrowed money used to finance these resources)

The cost directly allocated to the sale of one quart of milk is the price paid for the milk to the supplier – the dairy. In a similar perspective, the costs of a unit of production in a manufacturing or processing operation come primarily from the wages, materials, and energy. In a dairy operation, the direct costs of the unit of production – the quart of milk – would be mainly composed of these items. In the service industry, the primary or direct cost of the output is often the wages or salaries paid to the provider of the skills based on the time expended on a job. Legal, accounting, and other professional fees are usually constructed on a time basis.

The accounting reference to this particular element of costs, the direct costs of output sold, is the *cost of goods sold,* or the *cost of sales*. The amount varies directly with the sales volume. Costs of goods sold at the local supermarket during any time period is the price it pays to suppliers for the food and other consumer items sold to the customer. The remaining costs pertain to the ongoing functions of the supermarket – *payroll* for the skills of the workers, and the managers; *supplies* of bags, labels, record books, pens, paper, etc.; *services* of advertising, garbage, telephone, refrigeration maintenance; and *equipment* and *space* costs. Although necessary to the conversion cycle, they are not easily allocated directly to a particular sales transaction. They must be recouped in the differential between the sales revenues and the cost of the goods sold.

The accounting term for these remaining costs is *operating costs*. They represent the periodic costs of the available capacity of operations whether it is fully used or not. They tend to be "fixed" in nature. For example, rent is usually based on a specific amount of space. Its cost is the same, month after month, regardless of the number of products made or stored, or volume of sales occurring in that space. However, the amount of space ultimately limits the conversion and sales activity. The supermarket needs cashiers to handle the sales whether or not they are fast or slow, large or small, per customer. The cashier's wages are set on an hourly basis for the skill. But at a certain volume of sales, the skills of the cashier will be fully employed and so will the cash register. Capacity of these resources will be fully utilized. Another cashier will have to be employed along with another register to handle an increased level of sales.

Operating costs then represent the periodic or annual charges incurred which support a given level of capacity of the conversion cycle of the business. Since they do not tend to vary much within a wide range of sales, they are seen as fixed. The rent, and the necessary administrative costs — the contracted salary of the manager — are generally fixed in relation to sales volume. Advertising, transportation, and business entertainment are operating costs which are somewhat more flexibly expanded and contracted with sales. Nevertheless, they are considered fixed in the sense that they generally occur as a regular, and necessary, part of the operation of the business, not related specifically to any given sale. The actual volume of sales, reflected in the costs of the goods sold, indicates the utilization of that capacity. Ultimately, the level of use of direct cost resources — labor, materials, energy — is limited by capacity type resources.

COST OF GOODS SOLD

Let's say that you began a business at the start of the year, bought and sold many products, had some left at the end of the year, and incurred other expenses for your office. Focusing just on what you bought to resell, you could add all the bills for what you bought and subtract the costs of what you had left at the end of the year to determine the cost of what you had sold. If you had a business already in operation, you would determine the value of the supply of saleable goods at the beginning of the year (or any point in time), keep track of what was produced during the subsequent year (or a specific period of time), and record what was sold during that time. You could then determine the cost of sales during that period:

		COST
beginning amount of saleable goods	100 units @ $12.00/unit	$1200
purchased new resources to produce	100 units @ $12.00/unit	$1200
available for sale	200 units	$2400
SOLD	125 units @ $12.00/unit	$1500
ending amount of saleable goods	75 units @ $12.00/unit	$900

This simplified version of abstracting from the resource conversion cycle (1) focuses on the cost of short-life resources used up on the conversion cycle, specifically those directly related to the sale, and (2) assumes that the costs of those resources remains the same. Financing charges for the cost of borrowed funds are not included.

Consider that the business tasks of assessing available products for sale, determining costs and selling price, reordering, and assessing again occur in every business. It could occur on a daily basis, or a weekly basis, or every three months or so, depending on the business activity. It is practically automatic for the street vendor selling flowers, fresh fruit, or other perishable items. Each day this entrepreneur counts what is available from the previous day, estimates the new day's sales depending on weather conditions, location, season, and other relevant factors, buys additional goods to have for sale, and goes out to sell. When the day is over, the whole procedure will begin again. The local supermarket orders dairy products, meat and fish, and fruit and vegetables every couple of days in accordance with supplies on hand and expected sales. Canned goods and other consumeables are ordered every week or ten days since they last longer on the shelves. Special products might be ordered on an as-needed basis.

In the real world, all businesses experience changes in the costs of materials, labor, and energy almost all the time, and not always upward. A street vendor knows the change in the cost of the individual goods sold on a direct basis. As a company grows, and the numbers of resources transactions increase, the task of calculating the cost of each unit sold becomes impossible. What is available for sale at any given time becomes a big pool into which products ready for sale flow in and shipments representing sales flow out. With changing costs of raw materials and skills it may be just about impossible to track the specific costs of exactly what is being sold. The available pool of products changes in size and costs to produce each addition. Thus valuing the pool and what is sold generally involves a more complex accounting problem of abstracting costs from a continuous cycle of goods being added to the stock available for sale. The previous calculation only shows the change in volume and relates it to added production and sales.

FIFO AND LIFO COST CALCULATIONS

When the price of oil doubled in 1974 a number of large oil companies changed their accounting method for valuing the cost of oil they sold from *FIFO* to *LIFO*. These acronyms stand for "first-in-first-out" and "last-in-first-out." They label accounting methods to determine cost of goods sold. The former method essentially weights the unit cost of the oil sold by the company in terms of the purchase prices paid by the company at the beginning of the accounting period. The latter method weights the cost of the oil sold on the purchase price paid at the end of the accounting period. The two methods give a very different cost figure for the quantity of oil sold.

In quieter political and economic times, with basic resource prices relatively stable, the FIFO valuation method would give a fair approximation of the cost of the oil sold, based upon matching the historical cost to the sales transactions. However, with the purchase price of oil shooting upward, the oil company would be paying a lot more for oil toward the end of the accounting period. The average cost of the pool would thus be below, maybe significantly below, the price currently being paid for the new supplies coming into the pool. Therefore the FIFO valuation would understate the actual cost of goods sold. However, consider the valuation problem in terms of the conversion cycle and the accounting assumption of a continuing business. The oil company buys and replaces the oil it currently sells. FIFO valuation may result in calculating a surplus that was actually less than what really occurred during the accounting period. Hence taxable income may be "overstated." The consequence is possibly a tax bill for profits that were not really earned from the sales.

By using the LIFO valuation method, the reverse effect occurs on the calculation of the surplus. The cost of oil sold determined by this method may be overvalued, since all the product sold reflects the latest purchase price. Thus the surplus may be "understated," and the income taxes as well. Detractors claim that the profits are hidden by this method. Indeed they are if you just look at the specific period in which rising costs are occurring. However, the accounting perspective is on the ongoing business. That is, the oil is being valued at replacement cost, with the assumption that a repurchase of these resources constantly recurs. So hidden profits due to rising values of short-life resources on hand will in fact be reinvested. They are not continuous unless the price rise is continuous. They grow out of changing market values of resources already owned, not from values created by the uniqueness of the enterprise itself.

While both of these methods of valuation are open to criticism about fair representation and matching, one has to look at the larger picture of the ongoing conversion cycle of an enterprise. (See Figure 6–1.)

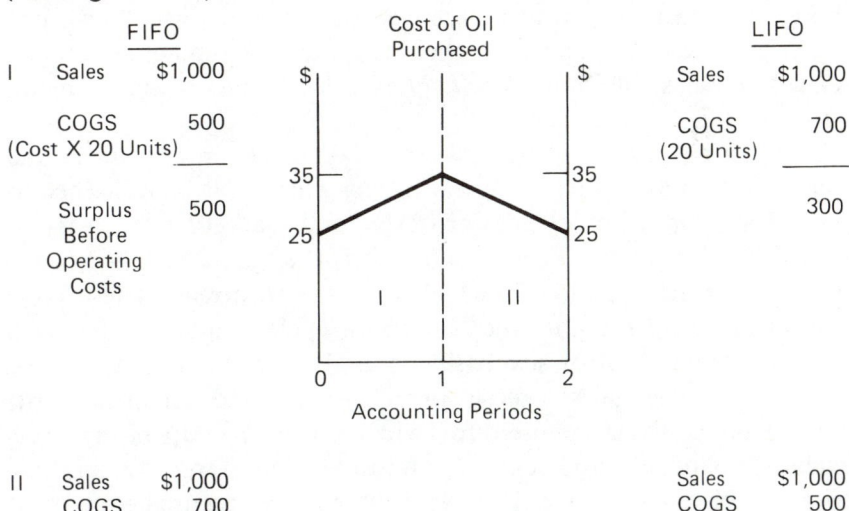

Figure 6–1.

Oil companies using the FIFO method in order to hide or protect profits from taxation when resource prices rise will experience the reverse when they fall. LIFO emphasizes valuation on the last-in (to the pool) cost. At the end of the accounting period, if prices fall during that time, cost of goods sold will be understated, therefore profits overstated. As a practical matter, the Internal Revenue Service will not allow a company to switch accounting methodology back and forth for the purpose of protecting profits from taxation.

OPERATING EXPENSES

In general, operating expenses consist of those costs of the conversion cycle that cannot be specifically related to the sales. Administrative salaries, for example, represent cost of skills needed by a business for general coordinative work. The price of the milk sold in the supermarket must include some allocation of the store management, but how much? The salary of the manager is more or less set at a given level over a period of time. The quantity of milk that can be available for sale is limited only by the refrigeration capacity and the delivery schedule of the dairy. There is no direct and calculable relationship between the costs of the two resources (milk, manager), though both are needed in the conversion cycle. Furthermore, you might say, the maintenance for the refrigeration equipment is directly related to sales, but not to *individual* sales. And the maintenance performed in one year may last several years.

Advertising the store and sales specials brings in customers and generally promotes sales. Operating costs can best be described as general support costs of administration and marketing necessary to the conversion cycle. For the most part, they are accounted for in the year or time period in which they are incurred. These costs may in fact help promote the conversion cycle at a later time, such as occurs when a lot of advertising is used at the start of a business activity. Nevertheless, these organizational and technical costs are usually fully accounted for when incurred. Operating costs exclude financing costs such as interest on loans and also exclude costs associated with one-time events such as selling used equipment or ending the manufacture of a product line. These costs are treated as not stemming from the normal operations of the business activities.

So too is income earned from investment of temporary excess cash, or gains from the sale of unused property or some other resource not normally bought for the purpose of reselling.

As indicated, operating expenses reflect the types of skills and resources used in the business conversion. A perfume manufacturer selling to consumers will regularly spend extensive amounts of money on skills and resources used in advertising and sales promotion. A manufacturer of precision tools will incur considerable annual operating costs for the use of specialized machinery and engineering talents. A distribution company, on the other hand, requires the use of warehouse facilities and transportation equipment for the goods and services that it receives and ships. Either it rents such facilities or owns them and incurs the annual expenses of such resources. Thus, long-life resources may be critical components of operating costs, depending on the extent of the production function in the conversion cycle of a particular business.

THE COST OF LONG-LIFE RESOURCES

In an accounting sense, when determining a cost of producing the sales, some portion of the long-term resources owned by the enterprise must be recognized in the total cost. The minimal selling price should at least return to the conversion cycle what was used up. The accounting profession has developed some uniform approaches to include the costs of using long-life resources in financial statements. The rationale behind these cost calculations, and the actual experience of the businesses using up these resources, may be somewhat divergent. But the rationale and methods of calculation serve the important function or providing uniform perspective and language, a basis for financial predictions and coherency in the preparation and use of financial information.

The problem of allocating use costs of the long-life resource to a specific time period is more complex than determining most other operating costs. And the difficulty in understanding the calculation is related to changing one's perspective from conversion and cash recoupment of short-life resources to recoupment of costs of long-life resources over an extended period of time. In the cash-flow perspective of the business manager, a long-life resource is acquired at a specific time for a specific amount. It will be used up during a number of years in the conversion activities. Sale of the output over time is expected to contribute to paying the original cost of the resource over time. This relationship, or expectation, reflects the accounting principle of matching costs to sales.

In the simplified example of the trucking business used in Chapter 2, a portion, one-fourth of the original expenditure for the truck, was allocated to each year's operating costs during four consecutive years of use. The resource-flow picture would show an outlay for the truck at the beginning of the four years, with recovery of the original cost through an annual charge (depreciation) for using up the truck to produce sales revenues. Regardless of whether the purchase of the truck was financed with a loan, or paid for in cash, the depreciation charge would be the same, because it is a calculation of resource use. However, if financed with a loan, the annual financial costs of interest will also be incurred until the loan is repaid.

In an accounting sense, the periodic sales generated from using the truck must be related to a periodic cost allocation of the original price of the truck. In a financial sense, since depreciation is a periodic cost allocation deducted from sales, but not paid out, it is a recoupment of the original expenditure, or obligation, for the resource. Depreciation is a noncash charge to sales. The primary assumption in seeing the depreciation charge as a recoupment of cash in the conversion cycle, however, is that that value of the sales is at least equal

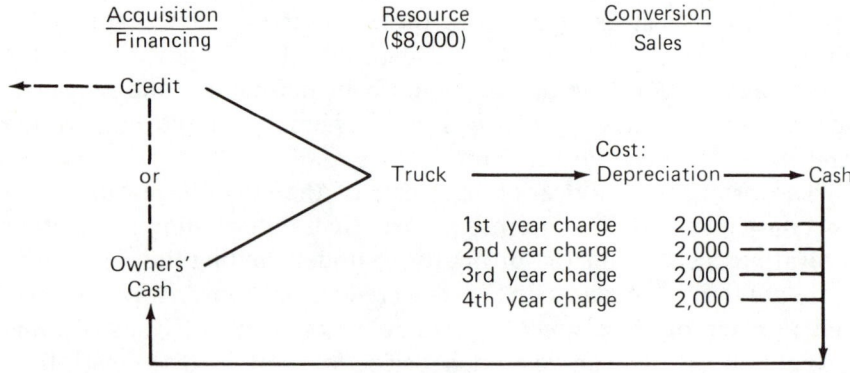

Figure 6–2.

to the total costs of resources needed to produce them. Otherwise, costs are not recouped. (See Figure 6-2.)

The calculation of depreciation is an accounting method for periodically allocating the costs of long-life resources. It would be impossible for accountants to sit down and figure out, with the help of the managers, the specific useful life of every long life resource in the operations of any and every business enterprise. Thus, a predetermined schedule of useful life categories was developed by the accounting profession and used by the IRS until 1981. At that time, the U.S. Congress enacted major tax legislation. The accounting bases for determining useful life was changed, through the consolidation of categories of resources and the shortening of the accounting lives. These schedules are not fixed in stone however. Where valid business conditions exist for calculating faster depreciation than is prescribed, the IRS handles it on an individual case basis.

Why are the tax people so involved? Because recognition of depreciation as an annual charge for use of long-life resources, deductible as a cost of operations, influences the calculation of the surplus produced by the conversion cycle. That surplus is the taxable income. Since periodic depreciation is based on the accounting life of the resource, if the latter is shortened or lengthened, the cost deduction from sales will vary. For example, if the accounting life of the truck referred to above were changed from four to three years, the annual cost allocation would be significantly higher than the $2,000. At five years, it would be lower. Surplus, the taxable income, would be less or more, other costs of operations remaining the same. In terms of the conversion cycle, the shortened accounting lives mean higher annual noncash charges — recoupment of cash (as long as sales value is equal to, or greater than total costs) — and lower taxable income. The financial effect of the tax changes was to recoup more cash in a shorter time. It was hoped by Congress that the shortened schedules would spur new investment and greater reinvestment of recouped funds in ongoing businesses. Thus, the concepts of depreciation accounting are highly subject to governmental tax policies as well as to actual economic life in an enterprise.

If the same resource was rented rather than owned, then the cost would simply be the rent paid for the right to use the truck during a specific time period. The resource is returned to the owner at the end of the rental period. No other obligations or outlays are involved, except for the rental payments (and maintenance cost, if that is part of the rental agreement). Many farmers hire harvesting services each year, rather than own all the machinery necessary for the production activities. Consequently, they have less invested in long-life resources. But the owner of the machinery, who provides the services, must recoup his investment in the rental fees, in addition to the other costs of providing the services. The point is that in one form or another, the cost of long-life resources must be accounted for in the total cost picture. In terms of ownership, depreciation is a recoupment of past expenditures. Rental is purely a periodic cash outlay. The lessee has no concern for accounting of useful life.

OTHER LONG-LIFE RESOURCES

As noted in earlier pages, long-life resources can include tangibles such as rights, trade names, etc. Depreciation is a label for the cost of using plant facilities and equipment — *tangible* resources primarily related to manufacturing and to commercial property. Other long-life resources such as patents, trade names, exclusive sale agreements covering a period of time greater than a year, or certain financial transactions where acquisition costs of resources exceed their accounting value, are considered *intangible* resources. The amount of the cost allocation depends on the time factor in the life of the right. Initially, if you paid for an exclusive right to sell a certain product in an area for five years, then the cost of that right could be amortized over the five-year life of the resource. In mergers, when a company pays more than the accounting value of the acquired resources the difference is called *goodwill* and is treated as an intangible resource. The accounting term for the annual cost of using intangible resources is *amortization*. In extractive businesses — coal, oil, clay, gravel, slate, peat moss, wherever a natural resource is used up — accountants use the word *depletion*.

BASIC FACTORS FOR DETERMINING DEPRECIATION

An estimation of the "useful" life is critical to the determination of periodic cost associated with the use of long-life resources. Physical deterioration and obsolescence constitute the major problems with recouping the value expended for the resources over time. Sooner or later a resource is used up in the conversion cycle and has to be replaced. Land is the only exception. It may change in value because of supply and demand conditions, but it does not depreciate. Useful life time depends on many factors such as regular maintenance, correct use of the equipment, unusual operating conditions, or weather conditions if a building is involved. Over time the resources no longer produce their benefits; the quality or quantity has fallen. Cars and trucks are used up as their mileage increases. Eventually they are sold or delivered to the scrap yard.

Obsolescence presents quite a different situation. A piece of equipment may be in perfectly good physical condition; but another machine may come on the market, a machine cheaper and more productive and reliable in terms of higher capacity and flexibility. The computer field, where each year brings cheaper equipment with greater computing capacity, offers a good example. In situations where obsolescence is expected to precede the estimated useable life, then a shorter life time must be considered for the calculation of periodic depreciation. Obsolescence may be an unpredictable but serious element in the conversion cycle, and accountants want to be very careful about the allocations most likely affected by it.

Almost all calculations of depreciation take into account an estimated *salvage* or scrap value of the resource. A piece of machinery like a used car will often have scrap metal value. And major markets exist for used equipment that still has actual productive life. Both cases are accounted for by estimating a future salvage value that will hopefully correspond to the end of its use and sale by an enterprise. Thus, as a company buys cars for its salespeople every three years, salvage value will be based on expected market value at the end of the three years. This amount is expected to be recoverable at the end of its conversion cycle, therefore it is subtracted from the purchase price to determine the amount to be depreciated during the conversion cycle.

Thus the basic components for determining the periodic cost of using long-life resources are (1) the *original cost of acquisition* (including transportation and installation) minus the (2) *salvage value* (the amount expected to be recovered when the resource is retired from use) divided by or allocated in some way by (3) the *estimated useful life* (in years) of the resource. The equation would look like this:

$$\frac{\text{Original Cost of Acquisition} - \text{Salvage Value}}{\text{Estimated Useful Life}}$$

It is important to emphasize that *acquisition cost* is based on historic cost, the original purchase price. Thus, *value* to the enterprise and *useful life* reflect expectations about use in the enterprise. Consequently, depreciable value to the new owner of used equipment relates strictly to the above three elements for each transaction.

METHODS OF CALCULATING DEPRECIATION

There are four basic methods for calculating and allocating period depreciation costs:

- Units-of-production
- Straight-line
- Sum-of-the-years'-digits (SYD)
- Double-declining-balance (DDB)

Units-of-production is employed where the actual usage is the main factor causing a resource to lose its value. Suppose a mold is made for the manufacture of a part. The mold will be needed to produce 15,000 units during several years. The annual depreciation will be directly based on use. The accountants' calculation will be:

$$\frac{\text{acquisition cost} - \text{salvage value}}{\substack{\text{(estimated total units of} \\ \text{production, e.g., 15,000)}}} \times \text{\# of units produced in the year}$$

The truck example in Chapter 2 illustrates a *straight-line* calculation; however, that particular discussion did not include the element of salvage value. In that simplified example, the truck was assumed to have a four-year life. Consequently equal amounts of operating cost for using up the resource were charged to (deducted from) the annual revenues of the truck rental business in each of four years. Under the *straight-line method,* equal usage over time is considered the main factor in allocating cost. The periodic expense, or charge, is directly proportional to the useful lifetime. Thus, the accountant's calculation is simply:

$$\frac{\text{acquisition cost} - \text{est. salvage value}}{\text{accounting life of the resource}} = \text{the annual depreciation charge}$$

The two remaining methods are called *accelerated* depreciation because they are calculated in such a way that depreciation charges are greater in the earlier part of the resource life than in the latter years. These methods were approved by the U.S. Congress in the 1954 Revenue Act. Basically, the methods recognize that long-life resources often tend to have greater productivity in the earlier years of their use than in later years. The truck, for example, will most likely be more reliable, hence more productive, in the earlier years. As it gets older, more mechanical problems will invariably arise.

The calculations of annual depreciation of both methods are based on the depreciable value multiplied by a changing fraction of the useful lifetime. For the *sum-of-the-years'-digits,* the SYD method, the accountants add the digits of the years of useful life. Given a resource with a four-year life, such as in our truck example, SYD base would be $1 + 2 + 3 + 4 = 10$. The multiplier is made up of the remaining life divided by SYD. In the first year it is 4/10 (or 40%). In the second year, 3/10 is the factor because four years are left. The annual depreciation then is equal to:

$$\frac{(\text{Acquisition Cost} - \text{Salvage}) \times \text{Years of Remaining Life}}{\text{Sum-of-the-Years' Digits}}$$

The *double-declining-balance* (DDB) is somewhat simpler. The multiplying factor is based on doubling the percentage that one year of the total number of years of depreciation represents and then multiplying the continuously declining balance. However, this method ignores salvage value for calculation purposes. Therefore, given a four-year depreciable life of a resource, the factor would be 25% $\times$ 2 or 50%. The accounting formula would be as follows:

$$\frac{(\text{Acquisition Cost} - \text{Previous Year's Depreciation}) \times 2}{\text{Accounting Life in Years}}$$

Looking at the four methods, we can calculate in more detail the cost options in the trucking business. Assume that the truck after four years of full use will have an estimated salvage value of 10% of its original cost of $8,000, or $800. Therefore, the depreciable value will be $7,200 over 4 years. Also assume that the company expects to use it for about 80,000 miles during this time period.

DEPRECIATION PATTERNS AND THE CONVERSION CYCLE

Ideally, the choice of depreciation method is based on matching, as closely as possible, the level of depreciation costs to expected use of specific resources. Thus, if the resources were expected to produce a relatively steady stream of revenues over time, such as in the power-generating business, straight-line depreciation would be the closest to the expected pattern of resource conversion. On the other hand, with a product expected to sell very well in early years and then rapidly decline, a diminishing stream of conversion revenues would be anticipated. An accelerated method would provide a closer match of cost with the resource conversion cycle. As already indicated, a unit-of-production method is particularly applicable when a fairly definable amount of production is expected from a specific resource. Added to these resource use dimensions is the obsolescence factor. The higher the risk of obsolescence, as in the computer and micro-electronics field, for example, the greater the need for an accelerated approach to account for the commercial reality of long-life resource use. The accountant's job of trying to represent fairly the cost of using long-life resources is no easy one!

In a very practical sense, the net cash inflows will be significantly affected. The method of determining depreciation costs will influence the levels and timing of cash recoupment for the resource and the taxable surplus. The accelerated methods will return more of the acquisition outlay earlier in the life cycle of the resource than will the straight-line method. (However, this statement assumes revenue-flows from conversion in all these calculations is enough to cover the total cost of the sales for any given period.) The accelerated method

YEAR	1	2	3	4
Units of Production	$1,800	$1,980	$1,890	$1,530
(miles used)	(20,000)	(22,000)	(21,000)	(17,000)
Accumulated depreciation (recoupment)	1,800	3,780	5,670	7,200
Remaining accounting value (unrecouped)	6,200	4,220	2,330	800
Straight-Line	1,800	1,800	1,800	1,800
Accumulated depreciation (recoupment)	1,800	3,600	5,400	7,200
Remaining accounting value (unrecouped)	6,200	4,400	2,600	800
S-Y-D	2,880	2,160	1,440	720
Accumulated depreciation (recoupment)	2,880	5,040	6,480	7,200
Remaining accounting value (unrecouped)	5,120	2,960	1,520	800
D-D-B	4,000	2,000	1,000	1,000
Accumulated depreciation (recoupment)	4,000	6,000	7,000	8,000
Remaining accounting value (unrecouped)	4,000	2,000	1,000	-0-

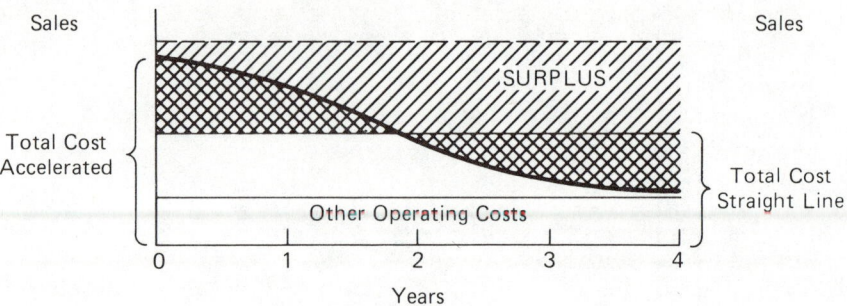

Figure 6–3.

reduces the cash inflow risk in the conversion time by reducing the level of future amounts to be recouped. It also shifts the taxation of surplus to the latter part of the conversion cycle of a resource, since the cost of using long-life resources is higher in the earlier years and lower in the later ones. Therefore, other costs being the same, accelerated depreciation means that total costs of sales are initially higher but lower in the future.

Graphically, the effects of the accelerated and straight-line methods show different levels of taxable surplus. (See Figure 6–3.)

Most companies will use several different methods of depreciation depending on the nature of the resources in use. Thus in the accountants' footnotes to the 1982 financial statements of Haemonetics Corporation, a manufacturer of blood processing systems and related disposable items, depreciation policies are stated:

Property plant and equipment is stated at cost and depreciated by straight-line method. Leasehold improvement (long term improvements on rented property) are amortized over the lease term or estimated useful life, whichever is shorter. Certain fixed assets used in making highly specialized products are depreciated over a 3-year life to give recognition to the factor of changing technology and possible obsolescence. Buildings are depreciated over a thirty year life and building improvements over ten to thirty years. Other fixed assets are depreciated over five to eight-year lives. Expenditures for normal maintenance and repairs are charged to expense (periodic operating costs) as incurred. Significant additions, renewals or betterments which extend the useful lives of the assets, are capitalized (treated as purchases of long life resources). The cost and accumulated depreciation amounts applicable to plant and equipment, which are sold or otherwise disposed of, are removed from the accounts and the resulting gain or loss is recognized currently (in the time period of the transaction)."

Note that where significant improvements or additions are made "which extend the useful lives of the assets" they are treated as acquisitions of long-life resources and depreciated accordingly. They are "capitalized" rather than "expensed," the latter meaning considered as an operating expense in the period incurred. A new roof on an old building is a long-life asset acquisition. It is a capital expenditure as are all acquisitions of property, plant and equipment. These resources are known as *fixed assets* in the financial statement. With the exception of land, they are always depreciated.

The sale of fixed assets, those long-life resources used in production, will either cause a gain or loss depending on the difference between the depreciated value of the resource and the selling price. The former is simply the original price of acquisition less the accumulated periodic depreciation. While the same accounting principle of determining the cost of resources in a conversion is applied to the sale, surplus or losses are reported separately from the normal operations of the organization's conversion cycle. Since long-life assets are used to produce some type of output, their sale is not considered as part of the normal activity of the business. Yet a sale is in fact a resource conversion and an important source of funds in the cash flow. It may have also a one-time impact on the periodic surplus or deficit.

FINANCING COSTS AND OTHER TRANSACTIONS

Up to this point, we have explored the nature of two major categories of costs: cost of goods sold and operating costs. The latter includes significant considerations in accounting for the use of long-life resources commonly referred to as fixed assets. The general structure of profit and loss statement appears thus

SALES REVENUES

less COST OF GOODS SOLD

Gross Profits or Margin

less OPERATING COSTS

Operating Income

Other Income and Expenses ⟨ Interest Expense
Interest Income
Extraordinary gain or loss
from sale of fixed assets

Foremost among the classification of "other income and expenses" is the financing charges incurred by an enterprise to support the resource conversion cycle. Interest costs of both short-term and long-term loans composes the interest expense. They are usually a recurring component. Where great amounts of financing are borrowed for businesses which employ high levels of fixed assets (e.g., pipeline companies, telephone companies, commercial real estate and the like), interest costs may be a substantial part of the cost of resource conversion. Nonetheless, interest paid is treated separately from the operating costs to show its financial origin rather than its resource origin.

Interest income usually arises from temporary investment of cash available from cash flow surpluses. Most enterprises invest excess cash until it is needed to purchase resources or pay bills that are coming due. Since this income results from changes in cash flow patterns rather than from the use of resources per se, it is generally looked upon as separate from the income derived from sales of the output of the company.

Other income and expenses primarily originate from the sale of fixed assets or other long-term investments of an enterprise. As expressed in the Haemonetics report, the basis for determining surplus or loss is the difference between the acquisition cost, (less the accumulated depreciation where applicable) and the sale price. Gains provide additional surplus subject to taxation. Losses are deductions from owners' investment. By separating the normal surpluses and deficits from the special or extraordinary ones in the conversion cycle of a business, the accountant attempts to distinguish the difference between the profitability of the ongoing business and the one-time conversions of long-life resources. This information is of considerable value to the investors since they need to relate their investment to the results of the normal pattern of the conversion cycle.

SUMMARY OF PROFIT AND LOSS STATEMENT

Basically, the normal or ordinary aspects of the resource conversion transactions are focused in the initial parts of the income statements:

	Revenues	*Costs*	*"Surplus"*
"normal" business transactions	Sales of Output	COGS Operating Costs Interest Costs	Gross Profits Operating Income
"other" business transactions	Interest Income Sales of Fixed Assets	Loss from Sale	Interest Income Gain from Sale
			Income before taxes

Income taxes are not a cost of doing business. They are essentially a sharing of the surplus, when there is one. However, owners' returns are based on *net* surplus or income after taxes are calculated.

While the above pattern may not explicitly appear to be in the accounting format of a particular profit and loss statement, the information base is the same. Those transactions related to the purpose of the business are treated as the "normal" sources of revenues and costs. "Other" transactions are (1) financial-interest costs or revenues or (2) "extraordinary" or one-time effects of the sale of long-life resources. The net amount is taxable according to the rules and regulations of the Internal Revenue Service and the state taxing authorities.

The remaining surplus, "income after taxes," belongs to the owners who may withdraw it from the conversion cycle, usually in the form of dividends, or reinvest it. Surplus not distributed remains in the cycle. Reinvestment of retained earnings simply recycles the net surplus into the business operations.

To complete the profit and loss statement format:

SALES

> *less* Cost of Goods Sold
> Gross profits
> *less* Operating Costs
> Operating Income
> *less* Interest Costs
>
> +
>
> Interest Income
> Earnings or Income (Surplus) before Taxes
> *less* Income Taxes
> Net Income after Taxes
> Changes from Extraordinary Transactions
> *less* Dividends
> Change in Retained Earnings

If there are losses, rather than surpluses, they signify that recoupment of costs through sales was less than the total costs of producing the sales. Consequently, there will be a net reduction in the investment in the conversion cycle.

7
THE FINANCIAL STATUS REPORT

Refresh your memory. Look back at Figure 4–5. Note again how the accounting profession abstracts and measures the accounting cycle from the activities of an enterprise. At the beginning of a period of sales, an ongoing business has resources which will be used in its operations. They will be converted into cash through sales. New resources will be purchased; payments will be made for previously acquired resources, loans, and other obligations. For example, your local supermarket reopens after the New Year's holiday. The business begins a new calendar year and a new accounting or *fiscal* year. The moment the door opens is a point in time. Food and nonfood items are on the shelves, supplies in the back. All are from "last" year—the calendar year as well as the accounting or fiscal year. Customers come in and purchase items; suppliers make deliveries. Employees start another workweek. Clearly the data and time form a reference point for an accounting framework superimposed on a conversion cycle.

If a new business was just getting organized on the same day, it might have some cash deposited in a checking account for making initial purchases. Cash is a pure financial resource, a medium of exchange. By the end of six months, many transactions may have taken place. Revenues may be generated from sales, and expenditures incurred for resources to be sold in the future. The end of six months, or a year, marks another point in time. The end also forms the basis for the beginning of the succeeding period's business activity from the viewpoint of the accountant. Measurements of unused resources at the end of a period of time are the same as the available resources at the beginning of the succeeding period. If a deposit of cash was made on December 31 giving a checking account balance of $3,400, the same balance becomes the starting balance for the new fiscal year. Both beginning and ending are accounting abstractions from an ongoing resource conversion cycle. They are nothing else.

THE BALANCE SHEET

Whereas profit and loss statements deal with sales and other transactions (not cash flows) within two points of time matched by the costs to produce them, the balance sheet assesses the available resources and how they are financed at any given point in time. So it is logical and necessary to relate the balance sheet to the beginning and the end of a sales period. The comparison of two successive balance sheets will show the effects of the intervening conversion activities on the resource availabilities and changes in financing during a specific time framework. (Review figure 5–1.)

The idea of "balance" comes from the fact that resource or asset values on the financial statement always equal the amount of financing for them. Value of resources, as discussed earlier, is entered in the books at the cost of acquisition. Either the owners paid cash for resources or they borrowed to pay for them. So this status report is always based on the relationship that asset value equals cost provided by financing sources.

$$\text{Assets} = \text{Financing} \begin{cases} \text{Creditors} \\ \text{Owners} \end{cases}$$

The sale of the firm's output or any of its unused resources means a reduction in the assets and a return of cash invested in the conversion cycle to the financing sources. A sale which results in a surplus between cost and price, as shown on the income statement, means a gain or profit to the owners. If the surplus is taken out of the cycle (other factors remaining the same), the equation remains the same. If the owners decide to reinvest the surplus in additional resources, that increase is financed by the owners. The equation remains equal, though the totals increase. If a loss is incurred in the sale of resources (the price received in the sales of resources is less than the cost of production or the depreciated value), then the financing sources have to absorb the difference. The owners lose their investment first. The greater the loss, the greater the possibility that the lenders will also lose their financing. When lenders cannot be repaid, bankruptcy usually ensues. Insofar as resources are acquired with borrowed funds, then the increase of the resources corresponds to some increase in debt owed by the company. The same is true with additions from owners' capital.

Accountants are hesitant to revalue resources upward since that is the fundamental effect of the sales activity. Valuation in the conversion cycle is generally determined by the buyer/user of resources sold. But where clear evidence shows that a decline in the value of a resource has occurred, an accounting adjustment or notation must be made and the corresponding effects shown on the financing sources where applicable. Thus, if the current market value of securities held by a company has fallen, it must be noted, otherwise a misleading impression of the resource valuation is presented.

Balance is based primarily on the facts of corresponding bookkeeping transactions. The total amount of financing must equal the total cost of resources acquired. The resources are changing in character, quantity, and cost with both the organizational emphasis and the output of the conversioncycle of an enterprise. Consequently, the sources of financing and the levels are constantly changing. The risk of the financing of the enterprise lies in the ongoing conversion of the available resources and in the decisions about acquiring additional ones. (See Figure 7–1.)

Figure 7–1.

THE STRUCTURE OF THE BALANCE SHEET

The guiding focus of the preparation and presentation of the balance sheet is the conversion framework. Consequently, the listing of categories of available assets starts with the most *liquid* ones, those toward the end of the conversion cycle. Cash is at the top of the list since it represents the end. The remaining categories are spread out to the most *illiquid,* the long-life, intangible resources. All the resources are divided in two groups:

- Current Assets
- Noncurrent Assets

The corresponding financing reflects the same breakdown with the following general structure:

- Current Liabilities (credit obligations)
- Long-term Liabilities
- Equity

Current refers to the distinction made in earlier chapter between short-life and long-life resources—the former being the expectation of conversion within a year's time. *Current liabilities* are those due for payment within a year; all other debt obligations are classified as long-term.

The balance sheets of most business organizations will show the categories of resources levels and their financing as follows:

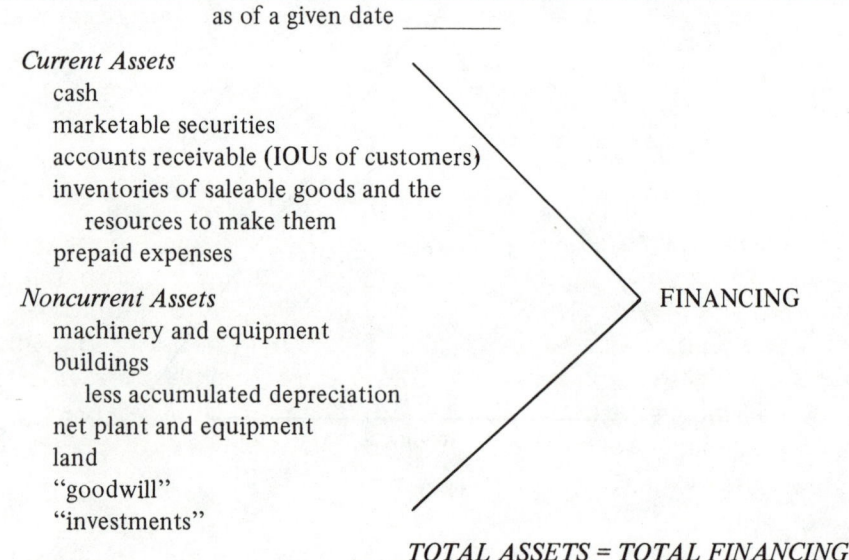

as of a given date _____

Current Assets
    cash
    marketable securities
    accounts receivable (IOUs of customers)
    inventories of saleable goods and the
        resources to make them
    prepaid expenses

Noncurrent Assets
    machinery and equipment
    buildings
        less accumulated depreciation
    net plant and equipment
    land
    "goodwill"
    "investments"

FINANCING

TOTAL ASSETS = TOTAL FINANCING

Not all business operations will show the same components. For example, retailers will show *inventory* a stock of resources composed mostly of merchandise ready for sale. A manufacturer's inventory will be typically composed of several inventories—raw materials, work-in-process, and finished or saleable goods. Unlike manufacturing, banking and insurance companies have very different compositions of resources. Their main job is to invest their depositors' and policy holders' moneys in income-generating resources. They are financing sources for individuals and other businesses. As such, their assets are largely income-generating financial investments.

Common to all financial reports is the arrangement of resources by liquidity priority and the separation of current from non-current nature. In the context of the resource conversion cycle; resource liquidity status reflects the nearness to cash, hence different levels of risk as shown in Figure 7–2.

Risks of Conversion

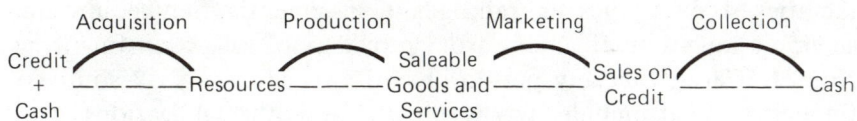

Figure 7–2.

Businesses begin the cycle by the initial conversion of cash and credit into acquired resources with the hope of selling the output at a price which covers the cost of production and credit plus a profit to the owners/promoters of the cycles. Note that the use of long-life resources involves greater risk of conversion to cash, since recovery of the original cost is subject to sales over time and obsolescence.

The financing sources for the assets ownership is divided into three major categories:

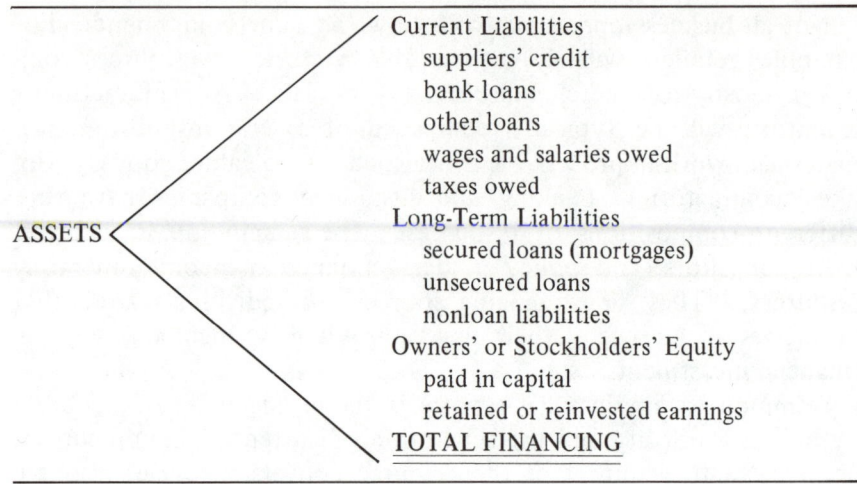

ASSETS
Current Liabilities
  suppliers' credit
  bank loans
  other loans
  wages and salaries owed
  taxes owed
Long-Term Liabilities
  secured loans (mortgages)
  unsecured loans
  nonloan liabilities
Owners' or Stockholders' Equity
  paid in capital
  retained or reinvested earnings
TOTAL FINANCING

What is true for the compositions of resources in different businesses is also true for the composition of financing. Retailers tend to have a high proportion of short-term credit, mainly from their suppliers, but also from banks. If they rent long-life resources, i.e., space, cash registers, then there is little need for other credit terms. Power companies have extensive long-life production (capital) facilities, so do airlines and railroads. Consequently, they require considerable long-term financing from providers of long-term financing. Note, however, that any person or entity owed money is a source of financing. That includes wages due and any other obligations, taxes as well as more formal instruments of indebtedness such as mortgages, bonds, and loan agreements.

Owners' investment is the higher risk financing since creditors always have prior claims to resources in the conversion cycle. Surplus belongs to the owners, and losses are borne first by the owners. Most lenders have no stake in the outcome of the conversion other than an interest charge for the use of the funds. Depending on the legal form of ownership, creditors may have access to owners for losses. Thus, in *individual proprietorships* (one-owner businesses) and in *partnerships* (shared ownership) owners are directly liable for debts of the business. The legal structure of the *corporation* assumes a separate entity from its owners. Likewise, the conversion cycle has a life of its own, whereas partnership dissolves when one of the partners dies or withdraws. The corporate entity is a legal fiction that provides limited liability for and transferability of its owners. Owners can only lose what they have invested in the corporation. Creditors' loans are made directly to the entity itself. Creditors have priority claim to the corporate assets ahead of the owners if the conversion cycle is unsuccessful. But regardless of the organizational form, the owners' financing is always at greatest risk to loss if the conversion cycle does not recover the full cost of producing the output.

Lenders often make *secured* or *collateralized* loans and in general seek a protected interest in the resources financed by their loans. A secured loan is specifically related to ownership of defined assets used in a conversion cycle. Through liens, collateral arrangements of mortgages, warehouse receipts, accounts receivable, and other assets, lenders protect for themselves a legal and conditional claim to ownership of unused or available resources of a business. Thus, when the conversion activity fails, they can enforce their claims of ownership to the resources they have financed and attempt to recoup their loan funds through sale of the resources.

Some comments about the language of the financing side of the balance sheet should be made here. The financing sources include *liabilities* and *stockholders'* or *owners' equity*. Equity is the accounting term for owners' financing as distinguised from debt, the creditors financing. Since Assets = Financing, subtracting the amount of liabilities from the value of the assets gives the *net worth.*

$$\text{Assets} - \text{Liabilities} = \text{Net Worth}$$

Net worth is in the accounting sense the value of the owners' interest. It is also referred to as the *book* (as in bookkeeping) *value*; the net accounting value of the resources to the owners. The book value derives from the past exchanges and financial obligations arising from them. It is not the value for which assets may be sold, either separately or together, as the enterprise.

All three terms, *net worth, owners' equity, book value,* refer to the same amount and to the same financing source. However, Owners' Equity = Net Worth only in the accounting sense. The owners' value of a profitable ongoing business (surplus-producing conversion activity) may be entirely different. That value depends on how new owners would assess the available resources in terms of acquisition cost and expectations of future benefits or surpluses from their conversion. Ultimately, value of ownership is only realized in a sale. A good example of market valuation is reflected in the changing prices of ownership shares listed on the New York Stock Exchange.

BALANCE SHEET ITEMS – CURRENT ASSETS

Cash

Cash is what is available in the checking account as well as the actual money in the petty cash box, safe, or the cash register.

Retail business operations usually involve a great deal of actual cash, though many purchasers use checks and credit cards. Credit card charges are redeemed by the financing institution within a short time of their presentation by the sellers. Cash levels reflect the incidences of cash flow transactions from operations as well as financing changes. The receipt of new cash from the sales of bonds or owners' shares means a sudden rise in the organization's cash resources. A few months later, the level will be down, after purchases of resources occur. When a company pays a dividend, a distribution of profits to owners, the cash level will suddenly fall.

Since cash is a medium of exchange; in and of itself, it is not directly a part of the conversion cycle. Cash levels are a momentary residual of receipts from conversion activities and patterns of payments for resource acquisitions. Because cash is an asset that does not produce income, a good manager will invest what is not immediately needed for purchases and payments in the type of resources which generate income. These investments are a temporary use of cash; they have to be safely convertible back to cash in the near future when needed in the business.

The next category of assets often found on the balance sheets of many companies, especially large ones, is the "near-liquid" investments known as *marketable securities.* As the name implies, they are highly marketable financial instruments which include U.S. Treasury bills, certificates of deposit (CD's) of banks, and commercial paper. They are all short-term debt obligations. The U.S. Treasury borrows on a short-term basis for its cash flow needs, and so do businesses. CD's (certificates of deposit) are issued by commercial and savings banks for both short and long term. Commercial paper is usually issued by very well established companies, and often with a guarantee of payment by a major commercial bank. Banks themselves issue commercial paper to raise capital for their loan operations.

Money market funds are also included in marketable securities. The fund managers purchase a mixture of these types of securities with their shareholders' moneys. Because these funds guarantee the redemption of the original amount invested at any time, without a prior notice or waiting period, they are highly liquid.

In general, the accounting for the value of marketable securities will note a variation from the cost and the market value on the date of the balance sheet valuation. A loss, if any, will not be known until the sale or liquidation of the investment. A short-term investment held to its maturity will return the principal amount of the loan even though its market value between purchase and redemption dates falls or rises.

The level of marketable securities found on the statement depends on a net cash flow position that shows temporary excess cash from the conversion cycle and financing transactions. Those periods of time will arise and disappear. These financial instruments have their own short-term conversion cycles. They have defined dates of redemption of 30, 60, 90 days or whatever. Most of them are bought and sold in active financial markets too. So they can be purchased and held for a short period of time. The amount of interest earnings they generate varies depending on the time held and the rates that lenders are willing to accept. The rates in general rise and fall with the supply and demand for short-term commercial credit in the economy.

Accounts Receivable

Accounts receivable are next on the list. They are debts owed by customers of an enterprise for past, completed sales. A company in effect acts as a banker when it sells its products and services on credit. The account receivable is evidence of a credit obligation of their buyers. The amount found on the balance sheet marks the level of credit sales outstanding at the time the financial information was prepared. More detailed information from the account books of a well-managed company will show the *aging* of these anticipated receipts. They are usually tracked and classified by a dating system: so much of the total due to be paid within 30 days; another portion, in the following 30 days; and so on. From such aging, cash inflow projections can be calculated. But equally important, customer bills that are overdue can be brought to the attention of the financial manager so that more concentrated efforts can be made for their collection.

It is from the aging of these accounts and company experience with collection of customers' debts that accountants can make a judgment of how much of the credit sales are uncollectable. Thus the balance sheet will note a portion of uncollectable accounts and give a net amount. The reduction of the value of these resources is a cost of business, incurred and chargeable as an expense, in the period of the sales. Another aspect about receivables that sometimes does not appear in financial reports is the portion of sales on credit to a small number of companies. For example if 40% of the receivables come from one customer, a substantial portion of the conversion cycle may be tied up to the fortunes of one enterprise. Risk of conversion to cash is greater in instances where sales transactions are dependent on one or a few purchasers than when it is on many.

Risk for the selling enterprise in this phase of the conversion cycle has to do with its judgment about the financial capabilities of the customers. The levels of accounts receivable reflect (1) the credit policies of the sellers, (2) the sellers' collection procedures, and (3) external influences such as the financial condition of the industry and the general economy. Riskier customers signal the possibility of greater levels of uncollectable debts. Allowances for doubtful collections have to be greater; therefore, costs of making such sales are greater. When economic times are strained, many customers tend to be late in making their payments. In effect, they are "stretching" the financing terms provided by the seller of the resources they use. The seller must then be able to finance a longer conversion cycle which often means increased interest expenses from borrowing. This stretching of payment terms by the purchaser does not in itself mean that the uncollectable portion of the accounts will rise, only that the selling company will have a greater level of accounts receivable in relation to sales than in more normal economic times. As a result, more financing will be tied up in the conversion cycle.

Since these resources are the financial obligation of other enterprises, they are often used as the guarantee or security for loans to the sellers. Because output has already been made and sold, the receivables are usually assets which banks are particularly interested in financing. And they can be and often are sold to financial institutions. The buyer may accept the full risk of repayment (*nonrecourse*), but not always. Such a sale completes the conversion for the seller. This special financing practice is known as *factoring,* and it is common in textile, highly seasonal manufacturing business, and import/export trade. Its history dates back to the growth of trade and commerce between northern and southern Europe in the late Middle Ages.

Overall, receivables levels reflect the types of businesses and the customer financing policies. Depending on the type of business, and the credit worthiness of the customer, the seller may offer considerable credit, or none at all. New businesses often have to buy their resources with cash until they build up both a record of their conversion cycle and a commercial reputation. Credit information is collected by the banking system about existing businesses for purposes of extending credit. Businesses often check with their banks and other suppliers or buy the services of credit rating organizations. The most well known of the latter is Dun & Bradstreet. In retailing, the innovation of the credit card financing facility meant that many retailers such as appliance dealers no longer needed to have their own credit operations. They could shift the risk and loan financing directly to the financing institution issuing the cards.

Inventory

At this point there is a major shift in the balance sheet items to the unsold resources of the company, *inventory*. For the local grocery store, it is primarily the goods on the shelves and in the store room. For a manufacturing operation, it is raw materials, products being made (goods or work-in-process), and finished or saleable inventory. The value of the saleable inventory is composed of the direct costs to produce or acquire it. It is intricately and directly related to the cost of goods sold on the income statement. The dollar value of inventory incorporates the valuation problems of LIFO/FIFO calculations discussed in Chapter 6.

The accountant has an additional concern when determining the value of inventory. If certain products are damaged or unsaleable (i.e., last season's shoe designs), then to not reduce the inventory value of what is available for sale misleads the user of the information. At times, certain inventory will have to be revalued to less than the cost to produce it. The difference between the acquisition or production cost and the revaluation will be an expense in the sales period that the adjustment occurs. Hence in accounting language, the inventory is said to be *written down* when an adjustment is made, and *charged* as a cost of goods sold to the sales of the period.

Prepaid Expenses

While inventory represents resources directly used in the output to be sold, other resources (mostly indirect periodic costs) make up the next category usually found on the balance sheet. These are *prepaid expenses* such as rent paid in advance, insurance, advertising, and other items. These expenditures are reduced and shown in operating costs when their benefits are realized in the following accounting periods. Thus, if the fiscal year of your local supermarket begins on January 1, and the annual insurance is issued on April 1, at the end of the fiscal year, December 31, there will be a prepaid insurance asset of ¼ of the value of the insurance premium. Three months worth of benefits will be realizable in the following year. The accounting picture is as follows:

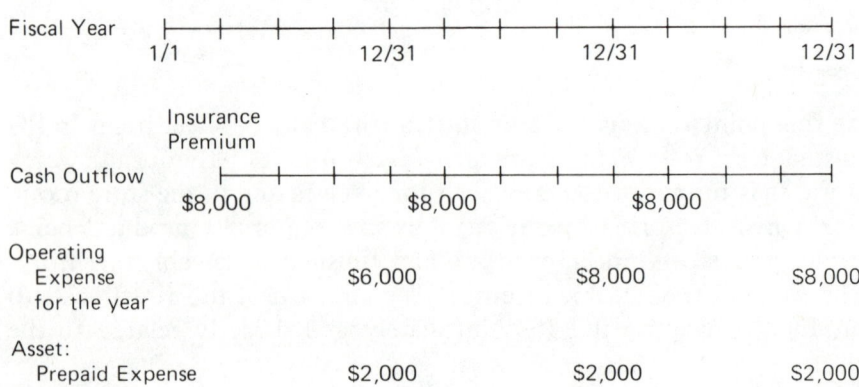

Insofar as a prepaid expense may cover a period of benefits longer than a year, then only that portion represented by the following year's benefits will be shown as current. The remainder will be a long-term or noncurrent resource. Suppose a company paid for 16 months of storage in advance. Their fiscal year ran from January 1 to December 31 and the rental began November 1. What would this transaction mean in operating and accounting perspectives?

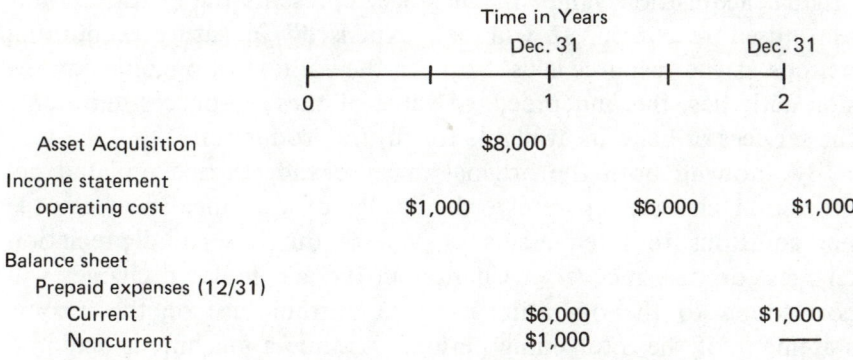

BALANCE SHEET ITEMS – NONCURRENT ASSETS

Noncurrent assets are those resources whose use or benefit derives over a period of more than one year. Our earlier reference has been the term *long-life resources.* In general these resources can be seen as (1) tangible and intangible, and (2) those relating directly to the regular business as differentiated from other resources which provide separate benefits.

Fixed Assets

Fixed assets are tangible physical resources of buildings, machinery, equipment and land. Their characteristics are:

- They will be used for more than one year.
- They are used in the regular operations of the conversion cycle.
- They are normally acquired for production rather than resale.

With the exception of land, each has a finite productive life. Each is used up in the conversion activities. The original or acquisition cost of these assets is expected to be recouped over time through sales.

The cost recovered is the periodic expense of depreciation shown on the income statement. Each periodic expense, or charge, reduces the value of the resource. The *accumulated charges* represent past allocations of the original cost to periodic operating expenses. When the accumulated depreciation charges are subtracted from the original acquisition value, the balance represents the dollar amount of unused resource. It will be "expensed" in future accounting periods as the resource is used up. In the context of ongoing conversion activities, the undepreciated value of these resources represents the services or benefits available for future production.

By showing both the original expense and the accumulated depreciation charges separately, the reader of a balance sheet can see net additions to fixed assets as well as the flow of depreciation charges, or cash recovery. Changes in the accumulated charges will correspond to the operating expense of their use on the income statement of the intervening period. Assume a machine is acquired by a company for $8,000. The accounting life is four years and it has an expected scrap value of $800. The company uses the straight-line depreciation method. The interrelationship between the balance sheet and income statement reporting is the following:

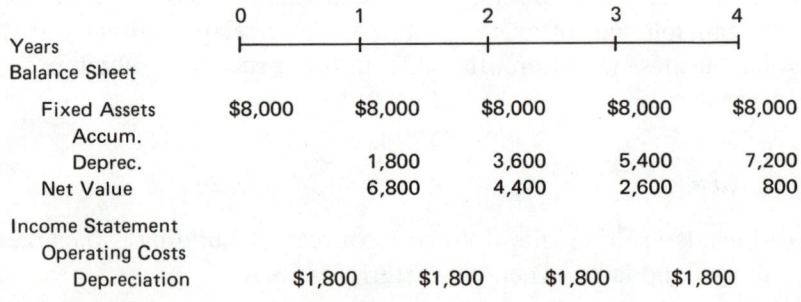

	0	1	2	3	4
Years					
Balance Sheet					
Fixed Assets	$8,000	$8,000	$8,000	$8,000	$8,000
Accum. Deprec.		1,800	3,600	5,400	7,200
Net Value		6,800	4,400	2,600	800
Income Statement					
Operating Costs					
Depreciation		$1,800	$1,800	$1,800	$1,800

If the company sold the machine at the end of four years for $800, then it would have fully recouped the outlay. The balance sheet would no longer show the machine. It would disappear from the accounting of the conversion cycle of the company. If the machine had been sold at the end of two years, then the accounting or book value, the unrecovered cost, would be $4,400. A price received over the undepreciated cost would indicate that in the conversion of this particular resource a surplus was generated. It would be treated as extraordinary income, since the company is not in the business of selling machines. Here too the equipment would vanish from the balance sheet, its conversion cycle being complete. A loss from a price less than the book value, would mean a loss in the conversion cycle, shown as an extraordinary loss on the income statement.

The use cost of long-life resources, with the exception of land, is recognized simultaneously on the balance sheet and the income statement under the varying title of depreciation, amortization and depletion. On the balance sheet the value is lowered periodically; on the income statement the corresponding reduction appears as a periodic cost. This recoupment of cost, however, unlike those of other consumed resources such as wages, materials and supplies used up, rent, and electricity, is not paid out periodically in the repurchase of these resources. It is purely an accounting cost, not a transaction, which expresses the periodic use of a long-life resource. At the same time, it is the recouping of part of an earlier expenditure in the conversion cycle.

In cash flow terms, cash, credit, or both, may have been used to satisfy the conditions of the purchase of a noncurrent asset. If the company used its available cash to pay for the machine, one asset on the balance sheet would be exchanged for another. Cash available would be reduced and equipment available would increase. No change in the basic equation Assets = Financing would have occurred. If the company borrowed funds to purchase the resource, the value of the machine would become a net addition to the assets of the company and the correspondent amount of debt would be added to the financing. Periodic cost of debt would incur added annual interest charges. On the other hand, if owners increased their investment in the company to finance the purchase of the machine, the additional asset value would correspond to their additional financing component. In a bookkeeping procedure, an intermediate step may have been an increase in cash corresponding to the receipt of the owners' new funds. Any combination of new financing will change totals accordingly.

In sum, each acquired resource is either financed by available cash in the company, additional external financing, or a combination thereof. The available funds are recycled from the resource conversion activities or acquired from outside financial sources or both. The ability to generate surpluses from the conversion cycle attracts the investments of lenders and owners.

Intangible Assets and Goodwill

One of the most interesting and somewhat more elusive categories on the balance sheet are the *intangible assets*. These are both nonphysical and noncurrent. There are two major groups. The first composes those resources which confer exclusive privileges or rights of use upon their owners such as trademarks, patents, franchises, and copyrights. These resources are generally characterized by legal and contractual lives. However, their accounting lives are not necessarily the same. They have to be treated realistically in terms of the use of expected benefits. A patent has a legal life of 17 years. Its economic and accounting value lie in its ability to produce income over that time. In a rapidly changing industry such as electronics, technological processes often have an actual three- to five-year useful life in the conversion cycle. New patents make others obsolete. Thus the estimated useful life of such a resource clearly offers a more valid basis to accurately calculate amortization charges. Therefore it remains as useful life on the balance sheet.

The other intangible resource is *goodwill*. It is usually an important element found on the balance sheets of enterprises that acquire ongoing businesses. This intangible resource represents the difference between the price paid and the net asset or book value of an acquired business. Something special about the business justifies the accounting rationale that the surplus expected to be generated by the future conversion cycle warrants a market value greater than the book value. Intangible characteristics or resources of the acquired business such as a good reputation and loyal customers, sophisticated and dynamic management, special marketing factors or technological savvy give the added income-producing value to the assets purchased. The expected benefits are incorporated in the special resource — goodwill.

Generally the accounting practice is to amortize the intangible resource, goodwill, over a maximum period of 40 years on a straight-line basis. Thus its value is reduced by 1/40th each year and becomes an operating expense on the income statement. However, if the earning power of the business was seriously curtailed, an adjustment would most likely have to be made to reduce the value of expected or unused future benefit. Many large or aggressively acquiring firms have found after their acquisition that the expected profits were not materializing and the recoupment of goodwill that was paid for the acquired business was questionable. It is not uncommon when a smaller firm is acquired by a large one, that the management of the former, which may have produced an efficient profitable business, leaves as it finds its innovative spirit hampered by bureaucracy and big business practices or limitations. In other situations, a bidding war among several buyers will drive up the price of the acquired company which may not justify future earnings. Business fads and shortlived trends produce the illusion of future profits inflating the current purchase value incorporated in goodwill. Acquisition prices of 1981 and 1982 oil and gas operations became a good example of fading profit expectations and asset values in 1983 and 1984.

On the other hand, in the footnote of the 1980 financial report of Gillette Corporation, $37,760,000 of goodwill "related to the acquisition of Braun AG (a European appliance maker) is not being amortized since, in the opinion of management, there has been no reduction in value." This amount was over 40% of the goodwill section on the balance sheet. The remaining 60% for other acquisitions was being amortized over 40 years. However, goodwill only represented a little more than 5% of Gillette's assets. The amount of goodwill varies with many businesses. A corporate policy of growth through acquisition is often the reason for a significant portion of assets labeled goodwill.

Regardless of whether an asset is tangible or intangible, the same resource conversion concept applies. And when the accountants look at the resources, their job is to help determine and verify the time framework that the business entity will most likely benefit from in using the asset. The concept of matching the costs to the revenues is the persistent thread in the accounting fabric. Determining useful life of long-life resources in a practical economic sense, is one of the most important measures of its application.

Long-Term Investments

Long-term investments are distinguished from other resources used in the normal activity of a business. These may involve the purchase of shares or bonds of another company, an exchange of resources, or special financing arrangements. Such investments may or may not be easily convertible into cash. The purpose for holding them is not to convert them as would be indicated by investments in current assets. As with any other resource acquisition, the accountant is concerned with cost of acquisition, benefit and expense from its use, and price received if and when the asset is sold. Long-term investment is an asset not used up in the normal course of the business. However, gains and losses are associated with these assets and must be accounted for. Many companies have a *joint venture* in which they are 50-50 owners with another partner. Their ownership is the investment in another conversion cycle. Insofar as that conversion is profitable, their investment increases in value. If the conversion cycle is loss-producing, then they as owners are subject to the loss. The value of the investment in the form of the intangible (shares) owned is being reduced. The owners of the investment have a share in the losses as well as the profits, either of which must be reflected in the accounting of their activities. Valuation of the ownership on the balance sheet must change up or down through the treatment of earnings on the income statement. The ownership share of the profits or losses is necessarily recordable.

Consolidation accounting is the terminology for the way the conversion effects on these investments are treated. Earnings (or losses) from investments are consolidated into the income statement of an investing company when it owns 80% or more of the other business. Earnings means surplus that is generated, not necessarily paid, to the investing company. The assets and financing are also added to the assets and financing of the investing company with a recognition of the 20% or *minority* position. Where lesser ownership is involved, the degree to which the investment cost is effected by profits and losses should be adjusted. With investments where marketable securities are involved, they will usually fluctuate in value with the changing effects of profits and losses of the conversion cycle. Consequently, subsequent changes in valuation can be noted where they differ from original cost of acquisition.

8
FINANCING THE ASSETS

RELATIONSHIP OF THE SOURCES

The sources of financing correspond to a list of resources owned by an organization or business entity. The "other side" of the balance sheet shows that either they were paid for by the owners or that, in a very broad sense, others (creditors) are financing the ownership. The sources of financing on the balance sheet comprise two broad categories: (1) *liabilities,* money that is owed or may be owed in the future; and (2) *equity,* money supplied by owners, usually with no promise or obligation of repayment by the business entity. Equity, owners' funds, also derives from surplus, generated from the conversion cycle, that is left in the business rather than withdrawn.

Any person owed money by a business entity is a creditor and therefore a financing source of the conversion cycle. The creditor relationship arises from funds being actually lent, or goods and services exchanged for promises to pay from the entity. For example, insofar as the local supermarket owes money to food suppliers for the goods that are on its shelves, the suppliers are financing the conversion time for those goods. The supermarket owns them and has use of them. Their cost is the supplier's price, which is the asset value. Their financing is the credit extended by the vendor, simply an unpaid bill for the same amount and possibly a financing charge depending on when the bill is paid. Thus, in an accounting sense, an Asset = Credit (Liability) on the balance sheet.

At any given time there are unused resources of the business entity with correspondent debts for their purchases, or the owner has paid for the resources, Assets = Equity. What is most common is a mixture: Total Assets = Total Liabilities + Owners' Equity. Since lending is essentially based on conversion time of a resource or group of resources, loan life is necessarily related to expected conversion cycles. In the construction of a balance sheet, creditor financing is separated and summarized in terms of short-term, or current, liabilities and long-term liabilities in the same way that assets are divided and reported. It mirrors the expected pattern of cash outflow over time. *Current liabilities* are those payments due within one year from the date of the balance sheet compilation. *Long-term liabilities* are those that are due subsequently. Lenders of funds provide debt financing, basing the cost on annual interest charge. Usually, but not always, the interest consists of a fixed charge per dollar borrowed. Some arrangements are based on *variable rates.* Interest may be explicitly stated or implicitly part of the stated price of resources bought on credit. Besides credit liabilities, *contingent liabilities* may also arise out of future events related to the business activity. They comprise a future cost, contingent upon an event or events. Some are more predictable than others, pension costs for example, others, such as litigation from product reliability may be less predictable. Contingent liabilities are those costs which can be expected in the normal course of the conversion cycle.

Owners provide *equity financing*. Unlike debt financing, it generally has no formal agreement regarding its return to them from the conversion cycle. Nor in most cases is there a specific contractual reward for the use of it as in the case of debt. Owners' rewards however come from surpluses generated from the conversion cycle. Since formal lenders' and other creditors' agreements are based upon repayment for use of their funds or resources *regardless* of the outcome of the resource conversion cycle, owners' investments pose the greatest risk of loss in financing the cycle. Lenders in fact look at the owners' investment as a financial cushion in the financing of the cycle of acquisition and sale of resources. When losses occur in the conversion cycle, they are borne by the owners. Consequently, the greater the risk of loss in a conversion cycle of a particular business, the more a lender looks to owners' participation in the total financing. Lower risk conversion cycles such as found in utility businesses — power distribution, telephone, pipelines — usually have a high proportion of debt in their total financing. In general, stable and mature businesses whose conversion activities are fairly predictable count on a greater use of debt financing than those whose cycles are uncertain or highly cyclical. In high-risk enterprises such as new business ventures, oil exploration, clothing

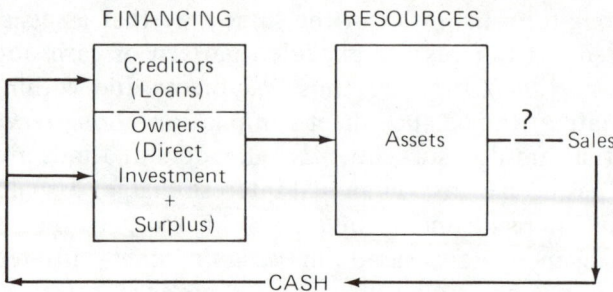

Figure 8–1.

boutiques and art gallaries, where the results of conversion cycles are unpredictable or subject to considerable competition, financing tends to come mostly from owners (See Figure 8–1.)

Business activity is a continuing cycle of resource acquisition and conversion. The reward for the risk that owners undertake with their investment is the surplus from the conversion cycle after all costs are paid. Repayment of a loan is not a cost; only the interest charge is a cost. However, loan repayments are a cash flow expectation and commitment. Expenditures for long-life assets are recovered from the conversion cycle through annual cost allocation of the asset value in the form of depreciation charges. Because depreciation is a noncash charge (a recoupment account) based on the original cost of the resource, regardless of the source of financing, it frees up cash in the conversion cycle over time. The owners can use it to repay loans, reinvest in resources for conversion, or withdraw it from the financing of the cycle. Therefore, depreciation is an annual source, a major one, for repayment of debt, *as long as* conversion income is adequate enough to cover all costs.

Repayment of a loan is not a cost of conversion just as the receipt of a loan was not revenue from a resource conversion transaction. Both represent transactions of the financing of an enterprise, hence elements of overall cash flow patterns. The cost of debt financing is the interest charge of the lender that appears as an annual charge on the income statement. The schedule of repayment obligations may be and usually is different from the depreciation charges. Thus, no necessary correlation exists between conversion revenues and the payment obligations of any specific resource of the enterprise. The difference between actual and expected conversion results of an enterprise and the contractual repayment obligations constitutes in fact the core of the problem of the risk of debt financing.

By using debt financing, owners *leverage* their investment. One dollar of debt plus one dollar of equity equals two dollars of resources available for the conversion cycle. As long as the price received from the sales of the resources exceeds the cost of the resources plus the interest charges, the owner gains from the use of someone else's money. However, an important trade-off occurs between increased gain from the conversion cycle and the owner's risk of using borrowed money. The possibilities are that resource sales will not take place, will not cover costs (especially sharply rising interest charges), or will be slower than the terms of repayment required in the loan agreement. Owners are responsible for repayment of the loans regardless of the outcome of the cycle.

VALUE

The question of value of the financing amounts appears quite differently when looking at the financing side of the balance sheet. Whereas the value of assets is "carried on the books" at cost, the ultimate value of the assets to the owners of business entity is determined by the sale price of those resources or output to other entities. The latter is unknown; it deals with expectations about the future and assumptions about buyers. However, most financing obligations implicitly or explicitly fix the terms of repayment in contracts. Dates and schedules for meeting payment obligations of principal amounts and interest on loans are usually established as part of a contractual agreement or in the terms of sale. While there are no absolute guarantees of repayment in the future, levels of financial credit-worthiness are reflected in the cost of the credit, the interest rate. The greater the possibility of nonpayment, the higher the risk for the lender and the higher the interest to compensate for the risk.

However, other liabilities, not necessarily contractual, arise out of the specific business activity. They clearly affect the owners' investments as well as the lender's position. The settlement of legal claims, tax assessments, or potential claims from product warranties or guarantees for such products as cars or home appliances are of this type. Companies often set up *reserves* for such contingent liabilities. The reserves are asset accumulations destined, they hope, to offset future claims. For example, consider the insurance industry. Uncertainty about future losses underlies the sale of insurance policies. Consequently, the insurance companies invest a considerable part of an insurance premium in the expectation that future claims will occur.

Changing values of foreign currencies offer serious risk to companies which borrow from foreign lenders. For example, Laker Airlines, a rapidly growing British company borrowed dollars to pay for American planes used in its international expansion during the late 1970's. At that time, British currency, pounds sterling, were valued at about 0.5 to the U.S. dollar. When payments started coming due on the U.S. loans, the British pounds were valued at 0.7 to the U.S. dollar. Since the value of the dollar had risen in relation to the pound, more of the latter were needed to purchase dollars for loan repayments than had previously been anticipated. Most of Laker's revenues were in pounds while a major part of its loan repayments were in dollars. Laker could not meet its loan commitments and went out of business.

THE FINANCING STRUCTURE

Corresponding to the *liquidity* (saleability) of the assets on the balance sheet is the immediacy of payment obligations. Financing sources are arranged on the balance sheet according to the timeliness of meeting payment obligations to sources. They are broken into two components — short-term and long-term obligations. The permanent investment capital of the owners, the owners' equity, follows. But accountants also consider and note the possibilities of future liabilities resulting from current operations of the business. Insofar as they occur, they could reduce the owners' earnings and possibly the equity in the future when they have to be paid. So between the known debt obligations and the financing of the owners lies an accounting recognition of potential costs contingent upon expected events. Payments of retirement income, when employees retire, comprises a future cost to be borne by the conversion cycle

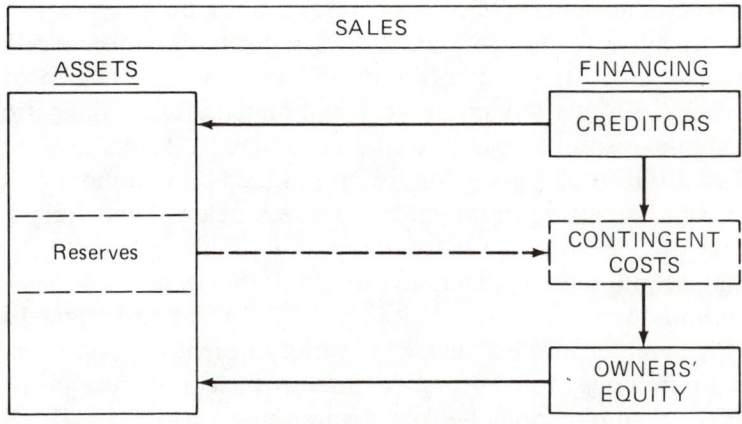

Figure 8–2.

and the financing sources. Consequently, it is shown in the financing flows (See Figure 8–2.)

CURRENT LIABILITIES

Current liabilities consist of all debts that must be paid within one year of the date of the balance sheet tally. They may include any portion of a long-term loan as well as the full sum of a long-term loan, if due within the year. Suppliers of materials and services are probably the major source of short-term liabilities of all business activities. Their credit is in the form of bills owed to them. Such debts are referred to as *accounts payable*, or just *payables* in the language of accounting. These are the reverse side of the same transactions that give rise to accounts receivable. Thus their time framework is the same.

Accounts	SELLER	Sale	BUYER	Accounts
Receivable	-------	on Credit	-----------	Payable
(Asset)		Accounting		(Liability)
(Lender)		Relationship		(Borrower)
(cash flow in)		Conversion Cycle		(cash flow out)

In effect, the seller exchanges a resource for the buyer's promise to pay within a future time period. The promise is not necessarily formal. It arises from an offer to sell and the acceptance of the resource by a buyer. A contract is completed and an obligation to pay for the resource results. Suppliers' credit terms are usually stated in a bill for the goods or are often based on commonly known trade practices. However, when businesses are new, hence very risky, suppliers often require cash for all sales, limit the amount of goods that can be purchased on credit, or limit the time for repayment.

Common to most current liability sections are commercial bank loans. They incorporate a very wide variety of lending arrangements: seasonal purchases of inventory, financing of accounts receivable (the delay in payment), goods held in a warehouse, crop loans, floor plan loans for auto and appliance dealers, loans for materials, financing of exports or the sale of imports, and much more. The variety of assets financed and the terms of the financing are practically endless since they are tailored to the various types of resources and the financing risks at different stages of their conversion cycles in different industries. Bank lending and company loans to officers and employees, evidenced by written promises to pay at a definite and determinable time in the future, are all included under the title of *notes payable*.

Because lenders are concerned with assuring loan repayments and interest on their loans, they often attempt to reduce the risks of conversion cycles by requiring *collateral* for their loans. Collateral is essentially a claim to or *lien* against a specific asset or group of assets that in effect back up a promise to pay with something of value. The lien gives the creditor exclusive rights to the disposition of the resources. When the borrower is unable to pay, the lender exercises his right to the collateral. This is particularly important in bankruptcy proceedings where secured lenders have first claim to assets of a business in order to satisfy their unpaid loans. Accounts receivable, for example, are a very common security for a commercial bank loan. Suppliers sometimes guarantee a customer's bank loan, as do parent corporations for financing of their subsidiaries. With smaller businesses, owners are often requested to personally guarantee commercial bank loans with their own signature and personal property.

Accrued payroll and payroll-related costs such as social security are part of current liabilities. Unless wages are paid at the end of the day, some portion is owed until payday. In effect, the wage earner is financing the conversion cycle. So depending on the day that the balance sheet is calculated, personnel charges will be due for payment. The same is true for social security (FICA) unemployment insurance, workmen's compensation insurance, and any other payroll-related expense, including the payment of state and local income taxes made by the employer. The charges are accrued from when they are incurred — the exchange of skills for pay — until the time they are paid.

Other accrued payments may include income and property taxes due within the year and dividends to owners which have been authorized by the board of directors. Gift certificates and coupons issued for redemption are a claim against assets of a business entity. Customer deposits, rent received, or advances on contracts, including magazine subscriptions are liabilities against which future services or products are to be delivered. Clearly, they are sources of funds for the business to use in the conversion cycle. Not until the product is delivered does this liability convert into a payment for the resource and disappear from the balance sheet. Savings deposits along with checking accounts make up a large portion of the current liabilities on the balance sheet of commercial banks and savings and loan associations because they can be withdrawn on demand. People and organizations that have deposits are not formal creditors, i.e., they do not have lender status. They have depositor status, a priority position. Banks are very carefully regulated by state and federal agencies to protect the participation of the depositors (a major source of their financing) and the integrity of the banking system. In addition the Federal Deposit Insurance Corporation (FDIC) insures bank depositors up to $100,000 per account against the possibility of a bank's inability to redeem deposits from the assets conversion cycle which is essentially loan repayments.

Lease or rental payments due within a year are also found in the current liability section. Insofar as a single lease payment is part of a long-term lease contract, then there is a contingent liability of the remaining payments if the contract is broken. This must appear in the footnotes of the financial statement in order to adequately reflect the liabilities of the business and the owners' investment. Probably more important is the nature of the lease itself.

The reference of *offsheet financing* for many years referred to the use of long-term lease arrangements as a substitute for ownership of a resource. The effect of such leases was to expand both sides of the balance sheet, but not in an explicit way. Assets were not owned and leases could be broken, thereby freeing the resource for someone else's rental arrangement. Since 1976, however, the accounting profession has differentiated between the type of lease that is essentially a purchase of an asset with a long-term payment agreement equivalent to a loan (capital lease) and those leases which may be a long-term relationship without any intent to own the asset involved, those meant to stabilize operations (operating lease). The former must show the rented asset on the balance sheet as if it were owned and the obligations (liabilities) of the rental agreement as debt financing. The latter treats the rental agreement in terms of current liabilities, rent due, and the contingent liability of future rents in the footnotes. In the financial analysis of balance sheets, investors note changes in the level of annual lease payments during both the current year and future years as well as the level of loan payments to be made in order to evaluate the significance of the cash outflow to be covered by future sales. As such fixed payments increase, the risk in the conversion cycle increases.

LONG-TERM LIABILITIES

Contractual financing arrangements that will not have to be paid for more than a year from the date of the balance sheet compilation are listed under long-term liabilities. Most common are mortgage loans or bonds. A mortgage by definition is evidence that a loan is secured by defined tangible or *real* property. What the balance sheet shows are the *mortgage notes payable*, the amount of promises issued and still to be paid by the borrower. As security to the lender, the mortgage represents conditional title to the property owned by the borrower. Transfer of ownership to the lender is conditional upon nonpayment of the debt, as spelled out in a contract between the borrower and lender referring to *default* provisions.

Security or collateral for a long-term promissory note or a series of them which comprise a bond (a long-term promise to pay) could be any valuable asset such as producing oil wells, stocks and bonds, a guarantee of the parent company, or equipment such as railroad cars. They may even be secured by a secondary claim as occurs in a *second mortgage* on the same asset. The second mortgage bond holder in this instance has a residual claim to the same collateral after the first mortgagor. There are innumerable ways in which bonds can be collateralized by the resources which they finance or any other resources owned separately by the borrower or even by a third party. The use of the assets as collateral depends on actual or perceived value and revenue-producing capabilities in case of loan default.

Not all long-term lending is collateralized. Debentures are unsecured bonds which essentially rely on the general financial ability of the borrower to make payments. They are lowest in the priority of debt claims as well as repayments. Consequently, it is usually large, well-established companies that are able to finance resources with this type of commitment. Since repayment of debenture bonds is based only on the cash inflow prospects of the conversion cycle, they pose a higher risk to the bond investor when compared to the secured bonds. Therefore, they also bear a higher interest cost, i.e., provide a higher rate of return to the bond holder than secured bonds.

What is most important about promises to pay in the future is the schedule of contracted cash outflows over time. Sooner or later these promises to pay in the future become current liabilities. Cash must be available for their repayment. If the resources which the bonds have financed are not producing the expected income, or if for any reason the cash is not available to meet the required outflow, the enterprise is in serious financial difficulty. It is *illiquid*. When payments are not made, loan contracts are in default. Creditors usually have a contractual right to demand full payment of their obligations. When that right is exercised, it may cause a cascade of demands for payment for other obligations. Under such circumstances a company will seek the protection of the bankruptcy court which allows the legal control of the entity to shift to a federally appointed mediator. The relationship of creditors' claims is sorted out and an orderly equitable plan for repayment of these claims can be attempted. Such plans often require the sale of some assets and the restructuring of the size and timing of payments due to creditors. In this way, annual cash flow obligations are reduced to match anticipated revenues. The company may be restorable to a viable operation.

Under circumstances where the business cannot be rescued by restructuring debt obligations, forgiving some debt, or exchanging some of it to ownership interests and other measures, the conversion activities are no longer financially feasible. The assets are sold under court supervision and the business is dissolved. Proceeds from the sale, basically a *forced conversion* through public auction, are then distributed to the various groups of creditors in accordance with the amount and seniority of their claims. If any funds are left after all the creditors are paid, then the remainder belongs to the owners. Owners are the last in line to recover their investment. However, in the usual circumstances of bankruptcy sales, creditors (except the secured lenders and wage earners) receive repayment of only a small fraction of their claims. The wage earners have special court protection giving them a priority as claimants.

The accompanying notes and comments in a well-presented balance sheet will list future payments arising from each long-term debt obligation. A schedule of such annual repayments gives other lenders and owners a clear picture of levels of fixed obligations that will have to be met with future annual cash inflows from the conversion cycle. For example, a new bond issue creates a stream of future payment obligations which may add to existing ones. The question then for the lenders is, "Will the annual net cash inflow from the ongoing conversion activities be adequate enough to pay off future obligations?"

The recent history of Braniff Airlines tells us a dramatic story about lenders' risks. In 1978 when the U.S. airline industry was deregulated, Braniff rapidly expanded its operations outside its traditional territory in the southern states. It acquired an additional 437 of the 1300 newly available airline routes. To service the expected passenger increase, Braniff bought 41 new airplanes during the following three years, (costing almost one billion dollars) and substantially increased the level of fixed payment obligations. A substantial portion of these additional long-life assets were financed by long-term debt. Unfortunately, anticipated results of the expanded annual sales and surpluses were not forthcoming. Costs of operations increased with the sharp rise of fuel prices in 1979 and 1980. At the same time, airfares were reduced to meet competition. In effect, the cost of producing a passenger mile of transportation increased, and the revenue for it fell. Overall revenues throughout the industry started to decline in 1981 and continued in 1982 as the effects of economic recession were felt. Braniff had steady and increasing annual losses from 1979 through 1981. In mid-May of 1982, 53 empty planes were parked at the Dallas Fort Worth Airport. The company was in the federal bankruptcy court. Though the planes were valuable resources owned by the airline they were not saleable at their accounting value (original cost less accumulated depreciation) because of an oversupply of used aircraft throughout the industry. Woe to the 39 banks and insurance companies who were owed over $700 million! Even the secured lenders had little possibility of fully recouping their loans.

CREDIT TERMS

Many different legal and financial terms and conditions define the contractual relationship between the borrower and the lender. In addition to collateral, some of the more common ones are *sinking funds, trusts,* and *call provisions.*

A sinking fund is a specific contractual obligation on the part of the borrower to make regular payments into a fund to retire or redeem a debt. A similar mechanism for debt repayment is effected through *serial redemption.* This procedure specifically sets forth what portions of a debt (by serial number or individual bonds) will be retired at specific future dates. Longer term portions carry increasingly higher interest rates than earlier portions, thus recognizing the risk of asset conversion and repayment over time.

Trusts are a common mechanism for providing an independent representation or agent of a group of bond holders of the same bond issue. Trusts are separate legal entities which, in effect, look after the interests of the bond holders (investors). The borrowing entity deals directly with the trust by assigning mortgages and other collateral and making repayments of principal and interest for distribution to the individual lenders/bond holders. If the borrower does not make repayments or fails to meet other conditions of the loan agreement, the trust is empowered to take legal action in the name of the bond holders. The contractual relationship betwen the debtor and trustee is spelled out in an *indenture agreement*. Banks often act as trustees.

A *call* provision allows a borrower to legally break a loan contract in order to repay a loan obligation. For example, a $1,000 bond may have been originally issued for 20 years, bearing an interest rate of 12% per annum. In its simplest form, the borrower has a contractual obligation to pay a lender $120 interest per year for 20 years for use of the latter's funds, and return the principal at the end of that time. The call provision is a negotiated condition of a loan agreement or indenture. It is insurance against falling interest rates and the possibility that funds may be available earlier than required to pay the obligation. Like all insurance, it has a cost. A *premium* (to the lender) or penalty (to the borrower) must be paid to the lender in order to buy back the contracted right to the future payments. It can be as high as the interest charge. The earlier the capability of calling in the bond, the greater the premium. So, a 20-year bond with a call feature of 5 years will usually require a greater premium than one with a 7-year call feature. But if interest rates have fallen significantly, it may be well worth paying the penalty.

In more recent years, some new bonds bore variable rate interest which rises and falls with changes in the bond market. Lenders can then benefit from increases in interest rates, but are subject to reduced earnings from falling rates. Borrowers are not locked into a fixed rate for the duration of the loan. However, their costs of borrowing are variable, and could be much greater than a fixed rate they would have paid when the bond was originally issued. The reverse is also true. The risk of changing costs of interest over time is shared; consequently, the need for a call provision would only apply to early payment.

NO INTEREST BONDS

Zero-coupon bonds have no interest rate stated on them, only the amount of principal and the date when it will be paid. They incorporate the idea that the value of the principal to be paid in the future requires a much smaller investment now at the prevailing interest rate.

Thus, if current rates of interest are 10%, a $1,000 bond issued now and due in ten years would have a present value of $386. An entity issuing such bonds could only buy $386 worth of assets, but would have a $1,000 obligation. The difference of $614 would be treated as an asset to be amortized during the 10 years. On the income statement, no interest charge would be shown. The annual amortizations of the $614 would be deducted, thus providing a recoupment of cash for this special asset. By the end of 10 years, the investor would have earned a compound interest (interest earned on interest) of 10% per year as well as be repaid the principal of $386. These bonds were particularly popular during the high inflationary period of 1981 through 1983. Interest did not have to be added to operating costs, though amortization charges were. However, amortization is a noncash charge like depreciation. It increases annual cash flow as a trade-off for a future one-time payment of principal.

THE CONVERTIBILITY OF DEBT

In a class of its own is the type of debt which gives the lender an option to exchange it for ownership interests. This type of debt instrument, *convertible debt*, has become a very popular mechanism during the past fifteen years. It is particularly applicable for financing growing companies. It can have an extraordinary effect on the cash flow patterns of the business enterprise as well as on the relationship between financing sources. Convertible debt is usually in the form of debentures, long-term unsecured bonds that have a subordinate relationship to all other debt. Furthermore, the interest rate paid on *convertible issues* is lower than what the borrower would have to pay without this feature. It is usually significantly lower. In any priority series of creditors, the unsecured subordinated lender is at greatest risk in terms of being repaid from the conversion cycle.

The more risky the conversion cycle, as those of rapidly growing companies, the more difficult it is to attract long-term loan funds with their fixed repayment obligations. By offering the lender the right to participate in the future ownership while at the same time contracting a creditor's relationship of preferential claim in case of bankruptcy, an enterprise can attract high-risk funds at a relatively low fixed cost.

A loan which is convertible into a specific share of ownership creates an alternative to a borrower's repayment obligation. The future cash outflow indirectly depends on the success of the business activities. If the resource conversion cycle generates more surplus, the ownership participation is more rewarding than that of the lender. Ownership is less risky than before, and the owners' position is worth more since the reward to the lender is limited to the interest rate. For the borrower, the conversion of the debt reduces cash outflow by eliminating the obligation of fixed repayments of the debt contract. When this happens, the borrowers' direct costs of annual interest payments are reduced. The principal of the loan, which would have to be repaid out of cash generated by the conversion cycle, is now a permanent part of the company financing. Former debtors are now owners/shareholders with decision-making power about resource utilization and owners obligations vis-a-vis creditors.

If the resource conversion activities do not go as well as planned then the debt holder will be sure to maintain the creditor status. Interest and principal must be paid. Owner's capital is still subject to prior claims of creditors' obligations. Default provisions can be just as strong as any other bond holder rights. So the investor in a convertible loan has it both ways but incurs a high risk in relation to other lenders and a low risk in relation to owners.

OTHER LIABILITIES

Other types of liabilities do not originate from loan arrangements. They may be a significant part of the financing section of the balance sheet in the sense that they are a recognition of certain obligations that will arise in the future. They must be indicated in order to show claims arising from the conversion cycle as a result of the way assets are used in the particular business. Hence they may reduce the net value of the assets to the owners or the owners' investment. Pension funding is a type of current cost of employees' compensation that anticipates future outflow of cash. To not deduct a charge from the current income to create a fund for this future obligation is to understate the full cost of the personnel resources used in the business operations. The same reasoning applies to the use of other resources and the need to anticipate as much as possible future liabilities stemming from the ongoing cycle.

When a company pays into a pension plan (noncontributory), the amounts are deducted from its current income as a cost of doing business and are set aside in a fund. The fund is an income-earning asset whose balance sheet counterpart is the long-term liability of accumulated retirement benefits. The latter are actuarially calculated since life expectancies of each employee are unknown. A footnote to the balance sheet should explain the accounting and funding policies of the company as well as the methods of calculating investment returns. A comparison of expected future benefits to be paid out with expected future value of the fund will show how much of the pension liability is *unfunded*. This unfunded liability is an additional cost that will most likely have to be paid out of accumulated past and future earnings when retired employees claim their contractual benefits. The claim is effectively against the owners' financial participation.

The same conceptual framework applies to future expected costs and potential liabilities arising from the provision of product and service warranties or guarantees. Thus, if an auto manufacturer provides a five-year guarantee on certain parts and against specific operational defects, it must create a fund for potential liability arising from its promises or suffer future earnings reductions from meeting claims which could be quite serious. In effect, the cost of an insurance policy has to be calculated into the price of the products sold and the premium set aside for potential claims. Aside from the funding of pension obligations and potential claims against product guarantees, other contingency situations may have to be accounted for. They include the outcome of litigation, possible loss from foreign revolutions or expropriations, nonpayment of loans, or any damaging events which, given the business circumstances, will most probably occur. The accounting principle is concerned with disclosing information about situations which will not be resolved until future events occur or do not occur. Thus if an event is probable and it will incur a significant outlay, the accounting should reflect it:

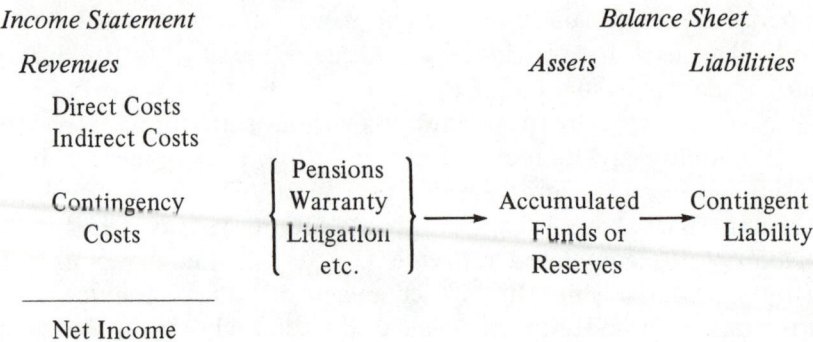

If a possible event may occur, then it need only be mentioned in the footnotes of the financial statements.

Setting up reserve funds (assets) for costs of contingent events clearly means reducing the current income. That may indicate the conversion cycle is less profitable than it appears. Thus, in order to determine if the past earnings of a business may have been somewhat overstated, an investor has to see if the contingent liabilities are adequately and reasonably accounted for by some sort of asset accumulation. More conservative management practices will protect against future events by attempting to fully charge now in current operating costs for their expected future liabilities. It is the idea of saving for the rainy day.

Risk is in fact the nature of all resource conversion cycles. Accounting for contingent liabilities focuses on costs that are part of doing business *now* but whose outlay will not occur until the future. The balance sheet in this particular area is future oriented. It essentially warns that the costs of the assets used to generate past income is most likely greater than was shown on the income statements. The future liabilities from contingent events are obligations of the owners, in the same way as loan repayments, though the specific amounts may be less definable or predictable.

OWNERSHIP FINANCING

Before delving into the accounting terminology and classification of owners' participation – owners' equity – a brief review of the overall

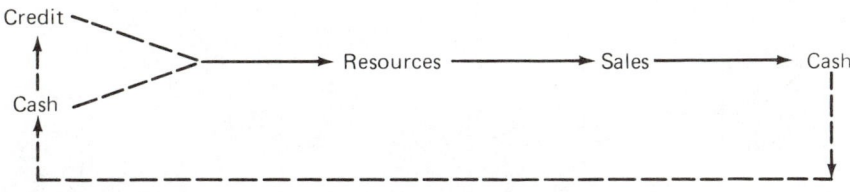

Figure 8–3.

financing flow of the conversion cycle is necessary for perspective. The ongoing cycle of the resource conversion activities of a business enterprise shows a time and transactions framework that requires financing (see Figure 8–3).

Continuous activity of a business involves buying and selling different resources at different times. Each has a different cash recoupment cycle based upon time needed to make sales, collection of accounts receivable, and the way in which depreciation charges are calculated when long-life resources are used up in conversion. Insofar as credit is used to finance a cycle, it would be most desirable to match the repayment of a loan with the generation of cash from the sales of the resources financed by it. Unfortunately, there is no way to guarantee the sale of resources as is clearly illustrated by the Braniff story. There may be ways to reduce certain risks in conversion cycles such as seeking long-term sales contracts, keeping needed resources at an absolute minimum (whatever that is), or producing the saleable assets after sales contracts have been signed. All this is done in businesses, where applicable, but there is still no guarantee about completing the future conversion transactions or completing them on a profitable basis. Thus financing sources are always at risk in the process of recouping the cost of the production of saleable resources. Lenders take a limited risk reflected in their preferential position to claims on the revenues generated from the conversion cycle and the resources used in it. Their reward is also limited generally to a fixed return or yield, the interest rate for the use of their funds.

Figure 8–3, which is the framework of this book, needs to be slightly altered to present the financing flow in the accounting framework (see Figure 8–4).

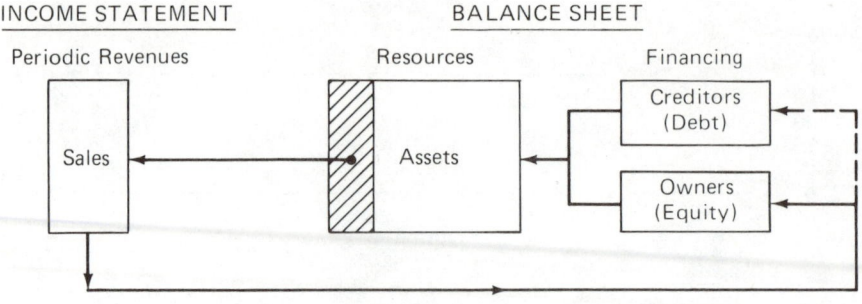

Figure 8–4.

When the sale of the products of a company returns more than the costs of assets to produce them, including the depreciation allocation and the interest costs, if any, then the surplus goes to the owners. Previously borrowed funds to support the conversion cycle are recouped through the sale and can be used to partially or fully repay the lenders according to the credit terms. If losses are incurred (sales do not return the costs of the resources sold), the owners' investment is reduced by the like amount. Losses reduce owners' financing; surpluses add to it, if reinvested in the cycle.

Because funds are derived from depreciation charges, a recoupment of prior outlay or commitment, they can be used by owners to repay loans, to reinvest in additional resources, or to withdraw from the cycle and return to their owners. A sale of resources completes the conversion cycle. In the case where the sale of production or long-life resources is not the normal activity of the business such as a factory, warehouse, patent, or product line, gains and losses are still accounted for on the income statement. Assets sold are removed from the balance sheet. The related funds freed up from the conversion are available to the disposition of owners in accordance with their obligations and objectives. Such conversions are treated as *extraordinary* transactions on the income statement. Based on the difference between the price paid for the resource less the accumulated depreciation (its net accounting or book value), the gain or loss is shown on the balance sheet along with the price received for it. A gain is taxable and a loss is a reduction of the return to the financing sources, borne first by the owner.

From the lenders point of view, the shorter the cycle of the return of their capital, the safer the investment. Time IS money! Time is also risk of nonconversion. As a practical matter, the return of the investment in resources varies with the use of it in generating sales over time. Cash flow obligations for loan repayments usually reflect expected patterns of resource conversions. Ownership participation with its attendant preferential obligations to creditors including the collateralization of loans is the cushion against the possible failure of expectations about completing the conversion cycle. The control of the resources is virtually shifted to the creditors when the conversion cycles fail.

OWNERSHIP FORMS

In sole proprietorships (one-owner businesses) and partnerships, (more than one owner), individuals directly bear the financial burden of loan payments. Business loans are in effect personal loans, there being no separation of the business activities from the individuals. The development of the corporate entity as a separate legal individual in the latter part of the nineteenth century offered limited liability to its owners. They could not lose or be called upon by lenders to be responsible for any more funding than they had provided to the business entity. The lenders had to look to the assets of the entity, rather than to those of the owner. The creation of an individual legal entity, the corporation, whose life was perpetual, and whose owners' liability was limited to the amount they invested, allowed owners to easily sell their interests or shares in a business. In the proprietorship and partnership, where the business and the individuals are indistinguishable, the business entity lives and dies with its owner(s).

Various approaches to partnership structures such as limited partnerships and subchapter S corporations incorporate features of limited liability. In the former, there are two classes of investors within the partnerships, the limited and general partners. As the former implies, limited partnership participation is protected from unlimited liabilities incurred by the general partner in the name of the business activity. The trade-off is that the general partner makes the decisions and takes on the greater risk. Most often in such partnerships, the general partner is the business promoter or has the particular business skills, and the limited partners provide the money. Return of the original investment and some type of split of the surplus is defined in the partnership agreement. Real estate, oil and gas exploration, Broadway shows, and more recently, research and development investments are organized or *syndicated* in limited partnership forms.

Equally as interesting is the subchapter S corporation. The word *subchapter S* refers to the U.S. tax codes. This type of corporation is a hybrid of partnership and corporate form. It allows taxation of profits to be based on corporate levels and losses to be treated as personal income which is the basis of partnership taxation. So the corporate entity exists for a going business, and the partnership exists for the activities which are not profitable yet. This special format encourages investment in new businesses by providing tax advantages to the investors at the high-risk state of the business. Loss incurred from the partnership is treated as individual and thereby deductible from individual income.

The key issue in discussing the ownership participation in an enterprise is the effect of failure of the conversion cycle from the decisions that the owners make about the use of resources and the financing of them. The following discussion of owners' participation will be in the context of corporate accounting.

THE OWNERS' EQUITY SECTION

There are two major features of the accounting treatment of the owners' equity section of a balance sheet. The first consists of the differentiation between *paid-in* capital, that which the owners pay into the company for ownership financing, and *retained earnings*. The latter portion is the accumulated surplus earnings (or deficit) from the conversion cycle remaining in the business at any given time. Surplus or net profit after tax is either paid out to owners or it is reinvested. The decision on the part of the owners not to remove earnings from the conversion cycle through payments of dividends to themselves is a decision to reinvest or to "retain" the earnings in the cycle. Retained earnings belong to the owners. Such financing is an internal source from the cycle itself rather than external financing from lenders or additional paid-in capital from the owners. Insofar as retained earnings are accumulated in a business they represent a growing value of the participation of the owners in the financing. More owners' financing means more resources can be acquired.

To review, if you subtract the amount of liabilities from the accounting or book value of the assets, you obtain the *net worth* of the owners' investment. Assets − Liabilities = Net Worth. By accounting definition, this is the value of the equity section, since Assets = Financing. Net worth is purely an accounting value, derived from the costs of the assets. Actual value of the net remaining to the owners after all liabilities have been repaid will be realized only through the sale of the assets, the completion of the conversion cycle. Thus the actual net worth may be more or less than what was paid for the assets. Net worth or book value are used interchangeably.

The second major feature consists of classes of ownership participation. This has nothing to do with the social order of the day, only the order of preferential treatment, i.e., risk of funding sources as they relate to the distribution of the earnings from the conversion cycle and the return of financing when a business is dissolved. Many financial reports, especially of large companies, will show *preferred stock* ownership as well as *common stock* ownership. The "preference" revolves around two ownership issues: priority of rights to distribution of earnings and priority of rights to return of paid-in capital, especially in cases of dissolution of the business. Preferred shareholders stand next in line to lenders in any distribution from the sale of assets *if* their preferential status also extends to priority over assets. The equation Assets − Liabilities = Net Worth to owners, is modified by the existence of two or more classes of owners. Thus, in the dissolution of a business, what is left to owners/shareholders is paid to them in accordance with their preferred status. Dividends are also paid first to preferred owners at a stated rate. They have to be paid to these owners before other owners can receive them. The trade-off for preferential treatment, however, is that the preferred shareholders usually give up their voting rights as owners for a priority in distributions from the conversion cycle.

There may also be classes among common shareholders. The principles are generally the same. The power to make major decisions is traded for prior rights to distribution of the benefits of the decisions.

But the common shareholder is in a residual or subservient position in relation to creditors and preferred shareholders. Further stratification of ownership interest means greater risk to the financing source on the bottom of the preference list.

Paid-In Capital and Par Value

The limited liability aspect of ownership participation in a corporation is expressed in the term *par value.* This amount, noted on a share of either the preferred or common stock, comprises the legal level of the limit of liability to the owner. In theory, if the owner paid less than the par value, he or she might be liable to the creditors' claims for the differential between the par and what was paid. Hence the par value acts as a limitation of liability. But with the common shares, it is somewhat anachronistic, since many companies have the par value per share set at pennies. The amount paid for the shares is many times more than the par value. A few companies issue shares with no par value. With the preferred, however, the par value establishes the amount of preferential distribution in the same way as the principal amount of a bond or loan contract. Dividends are usually based on that amount and return of capital, redemption or repurchase, is also governed by that amount. The common shareholders have the right to the residual, so the amount of the common share value does not matter in the distribution of proceeds from the sale of the assets or payment of dividends. As a practical matter, par value of common shares has little meaning in today's financial marketplace.

In accounting terms, receipts from the sale of shares are separated into two classifications: par value and *capital in excess of par value* or additional paid-in capital. The par value establishes the minimum price for which the shares should be sold and carries the history of the transformation of liability of partnership to ownership through limited liability shares of a corporate entity. Receipts of excess over par from the sales are shown separately and may vary per sale.

The classes of shares are indicated in the equity section along with information about authorization by the board of directors for their sale or issuance. The latter represent the shareholders in major decisions to acquire resources and encumber the corporate entity in its efforts to enhance the owners' reward from the business activities.

In order to be informative, a brief description of each class of the shares on the balance sheet showing their par values, number authorized, issued and outstanding, and total dollar amount of outstanding shares should be shown on the accounting statements:

Preferred stock — $100 par value; $9 cumulative dividend; 10,000 shares authorized; 5,420 issued and outstanding	$542,000
Common stock — $0.01 par value; 5,000,000 shares authorized, 1,657,400 shares issued and outstanding.	16,574
Capital in excess of par value.	4,104,602
Total Paid-In Capital	$4,663,176

In addition to the accounting for the corporation's sale of varying types of owners' participation, equity includes an accounting of the cumulative profit or loss from the ongoing business transactions measured periodically. Insofar as profits are earned, they can be withdrawn by the owners or left in the conversion cycle. Retained earnings, those profits recycled into the business, comprise the remaining source of financing:

Retained Earnings	$696,371
Thus total owners' financing would equal	$5,349,547

For analytical purposes, rather than accounting terminology, *capitalization* of a company is the sum of the long-term debt financing and the invested equity. It comprises the long-term components of financing sources.

There is no assumption about value in the equity part of a financial statement. It shows sources and amounts of owners' financing and classifications of owner relationships if there are different rights and preferential treatment among them. The financing itself supports the ownership of resources or may be used to pay debt. No specific resource is financed by the equity in the sense that the owners may have a claim to them in the way that secured creditors have a claim to specific assets. Owners own all the assets subject to claims of lenders, if any. Among themselves, owners may have preferential relationships to the surplus and net value of the assets.

Preferred Stock

The power of decision making is the key feature of ownership, particularly in the smaller corporations where one or a few owners have a majority interest. Since the owners are the risk takers in a financial and business decision sense, this power, a voting power at the board level in the corporate structure, is critical to ownership. It may be circumscribed by lenders' conditions when they put limitations on dividend payments or require certain levels of current asset financing or collateral, but the buying and selling decisions and the eventual disposition of the business are the reasons to be in business. They are the reasons for undertaking the risk. So the value of giving up this voting privilege is considerable. To be a preferred shareholder/ owner usually means to contract away voting rights to common holders in exchange for a preferential and more secure position in the ownership financing. Financial risks from owners' decisions that result in swings of earnings, changes in earnings distributions, and dissolution of the business activities are partially and disproportionately shifted to the common owners.

The preferred shareholder exchanges voting rights for preferential treatment in the distribution of earnings. They have first claim, which must be satisfied before common shareholders can receive distributions. Their claims are fixed by contract at a stated level and they are usually (but not always) *cumulative.* This significant word means that if dividends can not be paid when due at the end of a time period of business activity, i.e., the fiscal year of the company, they become an accrued obligation of the company. Accrued dividends, also referred to as *dividends in arrears* have to be paid first before any other distributions. If there is not enough for both classes of shareholder, the preferred owners will be paid first.

The dividend in the above example is a stated amount based on the par value. It would provide a 9% return to investors. The dividend could also be stated as a percentage as long as the par value was indicated. Preferred stock may also be *participating;* however, most of it is not. *Participation* signifies that after the preferred holders receive their dividend and the common holders receive a proportional amount, the remainder of the dividend distribution available to the shareholder will be further divided between the classes of owners on some pre-established basis.

The other major exchange of voting rights is for the preferential treatment in regard to assets in dissolution. This right of preference basically establishes that the common shareholders are the first to lose their investment in cases of a deficit situation in the sale of the assets to pay off creditors. Preference is through the shift of owners' risk of financing to be borne first by the common share owner, then by the preferred. However, this condition of preferential treatment is not automatic. It too is contractual in the financing structure and the particular share issue, as is the condition of cumulative dividend payments.

Preferred stock may have a redemption feature allowing the corporation to buy back the issue, usually at a premium over the par value. It might be in the interest of the common owners to buy back the preferred when the company is flush with funds, thereby freeing up the distribution of earnings to themselves. But the common owners through their voting power may also give the preferred shareholders the option to convert common share ownership at a stipulated price or ratio. A *convertible preferred* may be very attractive to the investor in the same way as the convertible bond, giving the investor the opportunity to become a common shareholder/owner when the company's finances and operations are stronger and more profitable. A convertible preferred issue would have a lower dividend yield to the investor than if the same were not convertible. It is offset by the opportunity to be a full risk-taking owner with rights to all the surplus generated by the business.

Common Stock

Common owners' investment, unlike that of bonds, has no specified security, no designated time for repayment, and no fixed claims to dividends as with preferred shares. It is divided into participations or shares of ownership, evidenced by the issue of stock certificates to owners. The certificate will state the number of shares on its face.

Based on the number of shares outstanding, it will represent a percentage of ownership. The owner is a stockholder or shareholder. The common stockholders' equity is equal to the amount paid into the company for the common shares plus the retained earnings. Asset – Liabilities – Preferred Capital = Common Equity.

There may be classes of common shares which create preferential treatment in the distribution of resources in the same way that the preferred do. They usually have limitations pertaining to voting rights and income distribution. The common shares of the Wang Corporation are divided in three classes. Class A are owned by the Wang family, Classes B and C are publicly owned. The voting control is in the hands of the family who are actively involved in managing the company. They control the major business and financial decisions through the voting structure determined by the rights of the classes of the common shares. Their particular investment was much smaller than the paid-in capital for the other shares, but it was made at a time when the company was a high-risk business venture.

As noted earlier, the board of directors (elected representatives of the stockholders) has the power and responsibility to authorize the issuance of both preferred and common shares of the company. The actual sale of shares may take place at various times and at various prices, depending on what investors see as their value in terms of risk of potential sale of assets and flows of surplus and dividends from the business. At any given time, the par value and excess of par will only tell you that a share sold to investors had an average price of the total amounts divided by the number of shares issued and outstanding. The bookkeeping records will show specific receipts for shares sold.

Shares may be exchanged for other assets, both tangible and intangible, or for services. Shares and rights to buy them at a set price may be used as additional compensation to lenders and incentives for managers. The ownership shares have accounting value because of an exchange for cash or resources and because of the effects of accumulated surpluses or deficits derived from the conversion cycle. Other stockholders through their representation on the board of an acquiring company would determine *value* of shares for the exchange in the purchase of another enterprise.

The common shareholders have certain legal rights in relation to managing the entity and its financial flows. The right of having a voice in the management of the operations of the enterprise is critical. Just in practical financial terms, the owners' capital is at highest risk in the conversion cycle. As companies grow larger, the owners' voices become more formalized through the election of a board of directors whose essential purpose is to be concerned with the overall advancement of the company and the stockholders' interests. Equal distribution of the gain from the conversion is also a significant right of the shareholders as long as they perceive it is in the best interest of the business activity to make a distribution. In order to prevent dilution of their equity, common shareholders often have a *pre-emptive* right to subscribe to new shares designed to protect their percentage of ownership. Finally, in the case of dissolution of the company's operations, they are entitled to a proportionate distribution of the assets.

There have been many court cases fought about the rights and influence of shareholders who have a small (minority) interest. Courts have generally protected their position when the major stockholders have taken actions which would be disproportionately beneficial to the latter. The key components of ownership are the right to distribution of assets and the powers of making decisions offset by the risks that they will not benefit the owners/shareholders. The division of ownership into classes and protection of minority shareholders reflects these issues that ultimately decide value or protection of investment to the owner.

DIVIDENDS

Dividends are the distribution of assets to shareholders. They are not limited to the accounting surplus. They may also be a return of paid-in capital or may be in the form of additional ownership participation. Payments of current or accumulated earnings are usually referred to as *cash dividends,* while *liquidating dividends* refer to distributions of previously paid capital. A *stock dividend* is the payment of shares instead of cash. From the accounting viewpoint, the retained earnings section is reduced by the dollar value of the stock to be distributed. The par value and the paid-in sections are increased by a like amount. This is a method of retaining equity capital while rewarding owners for their risk.

Sometimes a company will transfer its ownership of a subsidiary company directly to its shareholders. Shareholders will receive new shares on a basis proportionate to their holdings. Thus a transfer of assets and ownership takes place. It derives from previous ownership. In a similar sense, there is no reason why a camera company cannot give cameras to its shareholders, on a proportionate basis, as a dividend. An owner with 1,000 shares might however prefer cash. It is also possible that a majority shareholder may forego the payment of his or her proportionate share of dividends while voting for the distribution to other shareholders. This preserves investment capital which the majority owner may feel is more important to have in the firm, even if future benefits are shared equally by everyone. Hugh Hefner, the 72% of Playboy Enterprises, whose shares are traded on the New York Stock Exchange, has taken this action at many annual meetings.

9
THE MEASUREMENTS OF CHANGING BALANCE SHEETS

If you compare a sequence of income statements, you can track a periodic measure of levels of sales and changes of component costs to produce them. The income statement is a cost-oriented document which has no particular time reference to the decisions which affected the flow of resources used nor to their financing in the conversion cycle. Since the balance sheet is a measure of available resources and their financing at an instant of time, changes in its composition between the beginning, and the end of a sales period show resource acquisition, disposal, and financing decisions. A large part of balance sheet changes do not relate to the sales transaction in a given time period bracketed by two balance sheets. Many are the acquisitions of resources for future conversion and changes in the financing arrangements both from the past and for the future conversion cycle. For example, profits generated from current sales belong to the owners. They accumulate in the cycle as retained earnings on the balance sheet, if they are not paid out to the owners as dividends. This flow of additional financing generated from the conversion cycle can be used to acquire both short- and long-life resources, or to pay down past debt obligations.

STATEMENT OF CHANGES IN THE FINANCIAL POSITION

The accounting statement which measures these changes in resource availabilities and their financing between two consecutive balance sheet tallies is a *statement of changes in the financial position,* sometimes referred to as a *source and use of funds statement.* The accounting profession has only been required to make this report since 1971. It complements and explains the balance sheet comparisons of a fiscal period by showing how funds were specifically generated from the conversion cycle and from financing sources, and how they were

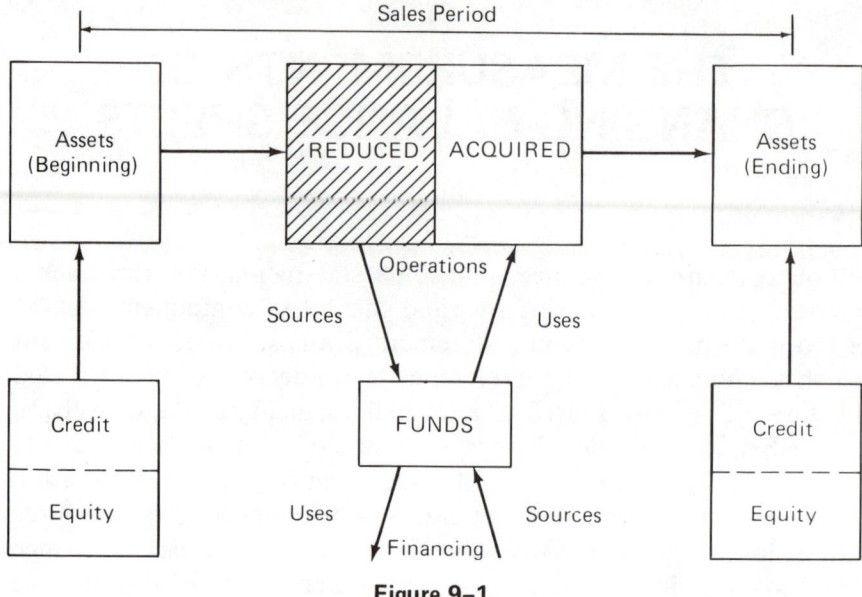

Figure 9–1.

used by an enterprise. It highlights (1) the investment in longer term productive capacity of the entity, and (2) the working capital health of the entity (the changes in the levels of current assets, which are the short-term cash generating resources).

Changes in the levels of the balance sheet measurements between the beginning and the end of a sales period focus on the future capability of the entity to continue its conversion activity — to meet financial obligations and to produce saleable resources. As seen in Figure 9–1, *funds* comprise both the cash flowing from operations as well as loans and cash arising from the sales of new equity shares. As long as sales revenues cover all costs of the output sold, including depreciation charges, then they are a recoupment of earlier expenditures from the conversion cycle. Depreciation as a charge to recoup prior investment outlays, represents a major source of cash flowing from operations since it is a noncash charge to sales during an operating period. Depreciation is in fact a reduction (using up) of assets, and like any reduction of assets through sales, it gives rise to cash inflows. Since this inflow represents the using up of production resources, it implies that they will have to be replaced at some point in the future.

Annual surpluses are also a major source, but they represent new funds generated internally from the conversion cycle. When retained they add asset acquisition potential to the cycle. Insofar as a loss is incurred from the sales of assets, previous investment in them was not fully recouped from the conversion cycle. The amount of the loss translates into a reduction of reuseable funds and an equivalent reduction of the owners' investment in the accounting period. It is important to note that both the generation of surplus and depreciation do not necessarily provide immediate cash from operations unless all sales are on a cash basis. Sales made on short-term credit do however eventually provide cash when payment is made by the buyer.

Increases in levels of loans add to funds available to acquire additional assets. When loans are repaid, the opposite effect is true. Equity funds increase through purchases of shares by investors (paid-in capital) and through the accumulation of periodic surplus or retained earnings. New funds from purchases of equity interests are *external* to the conversion cycle and are shown as external financing sources in the diagram. In sum, external funding augments the ability of an enterprise to acquire assets for future conversion and generates surplus for the owners. Alternatively it may be used to restructure the financing by reducing debt or refinancing short-term debt with long-term debt.

INTERNAL AND EXTERNAL FINANCING SOURCES

The changes in the financial position (or condition) statement focuses on the *net* changes of resource levels and financing components to show how funds were used and *generated* during a specific period of operations. In general, funds are generated from the conversion cycle (1) internally by selling assets and (2) externally from increases in credit and owners' financing. Funds are *used* for (1) the acquisition of assets, (2) the repayments of loans and reduction of other obligations, and (3) the withdrawal of owners' capital and surplus through dividend payments and repurchases of equity shares.

This accounting statement combines the potential net cash flows expressed in and derived from the income statement with changes in the composition of the balance sheet items. The most common format is the following:

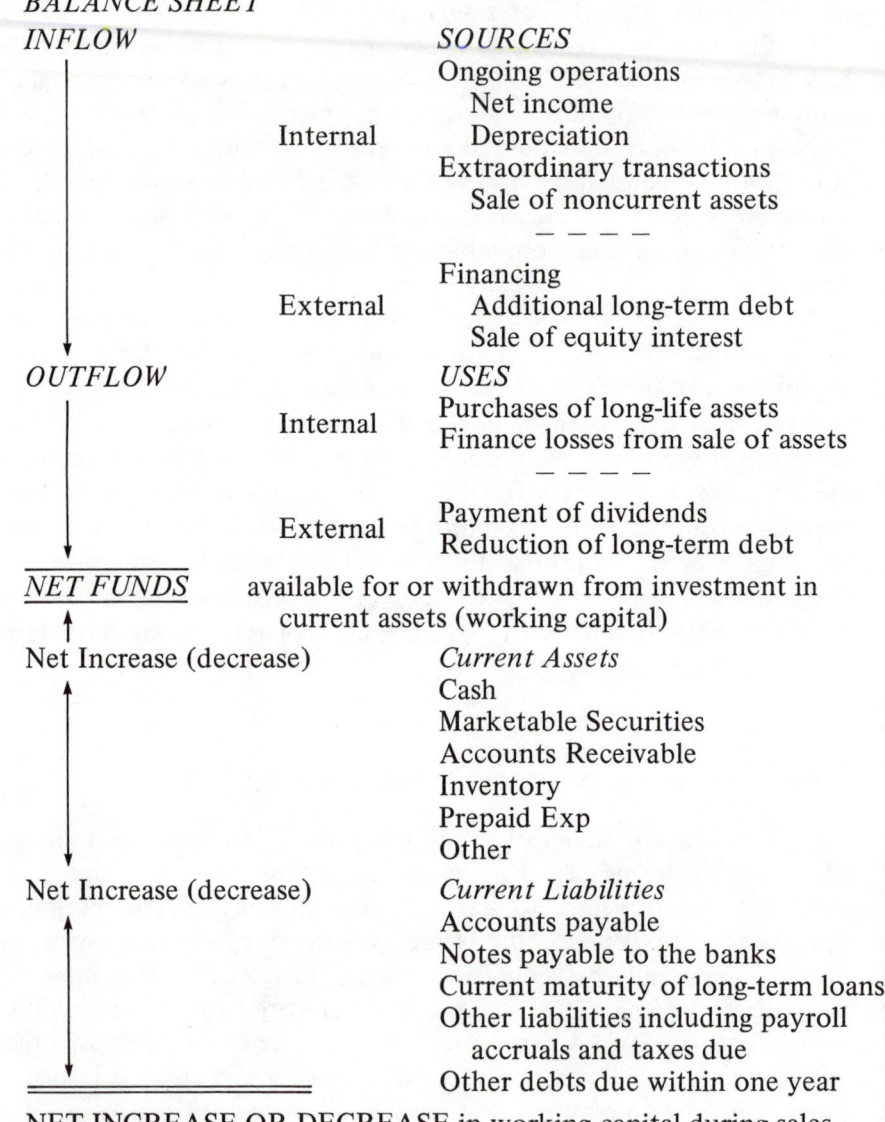

BALANCE SHEET

INFLOW   *SOURCES*

Ongoing operations
Net income
Internal   Depreciation
Extraordinary transactions
Sale of noncurrent assets

Financing
External   Additional long-term debt
Sale of equity interest

OUTFLOW   *USES*

Internal   Purchases of long-life assets
Finance losses from sale of assets

External   Payment of dividends
Reduction of long-term debt

NET FUNDS   available for or withdrawn from investment in current assets (working capital)

Net Increase (decrease)   *Current Assets*
Cash
Marketable Securities
Accounts Receivable
Inventory
Prepaid Exp
Other

Net Increase (decrease)   *Current Liabilities*
Accounts payable
Notes payable to the banks
Current maturity of long-term loans
Other liabilities including payroll accruals and taxes due
Other debts due within one year

NET INCREASE OR DECREASE in working capital during sales period.

The statement is designed to give a picture of management handling of the financing of the conversion and their decisions regarding the use of resources during a specific period of the conversion cycle. The format may vary but the purpose is to provide information to creditors and investors about changes in the current assets levels in relation to the acquisition and disposition of long-life assets. Financial information from the 1982 annual report of Haemonetics Corporation offers a good example of these transactions (see Figure 9–2).

In this growing company, whose sales increased from almost $24 million in 1981 to $30 million in 1982, changes in the balance sheet items indicate that the rapid expansion of the conversion cycle is requiring considerable external financing. Major internally generated sources from surplus and depreciation were over $3.5 million in 1982, but the sum is inadequate to finance both expansion of $2.12 million for manufacturing capacity and the changes in current assets of inventories and accounts receivable needed to support increased sales. These amounted to $2.65 million. The sharp rise in temporary cash investments (marketable securities) resulted from the sale of common stock which netted the company $5.9 million. This additional financing was partially used to support the asset growth. The remainder, the temporary investment, will be used for continued expansion of plant and equipment and working capital in the operations of the following year. The *significant* changes in resources and financing levels during the 1982 period were the following:

USES ($ millions)		*SOURCES ($ millions)*	
Long-life Assets:		Operations:	
Plant and Equipment	$2.12	Net income	$2.69
		Depreciation	.84
Available for current assets (working capital)			
	$1.41		
Current Assets:		External Funds:	
Accounts receivable	2.01	Accounts payable	
		(suppliers' credits)	.43
Inventory	1.64		
Additional financing required			
	($1.81)		
Temporary Cash		Equity	5.87
Investment	4.63		

Consolidated Statements of Changes in Financial Position
Haemonetics Corporation and Subsidiaries
(In thousands)

	Years Ended March 31,		
	1980	1981	1982
Working capital was provided by:			
Net income	$1,697	$2,196	$2,689
Additional charges to operations not requiring the use of working capital:			
Deferred taxes	253	264	297
Depreciation and amortization of property, plant and equipment	419	569	840
Amortization of common stock awards	21	36	53
Working capital provided by operations	2,390	3,065	3,879
Conversion of long-term debt to common stock	350	—	—
Proceeds from long-term debt	—	3,600	15
Proceeds from sale of common stock, net of related expense	3,744	—	5,875
Proceeds from stock issued under Equity Sharing Plan and option plans	152	162	111
Total working capital provided	6,636	6,827	9,880
Working capital was applied to:			
Reduction of long-term debt	511	248	240
Retirement of long-term debt with common stock	350	—	—
Net additions to property, plant and equipment	942	5,038	2,118
Other—net	10	108	(5
Total working capital applied	1,813	5,394	2,353
Increase in working capital	$4,823	$1,433	$7,527
Changes in elements of working capital:			
Increase (decrease) in current assets:			
Cash	$ (121)	$ 253	$ (106
Temporary cash investments	2,442	(720)	4,632
Accounts receivable	1,709	1,342	2,011
Inventories	1,394	1,381	1,641
Other current assets	3	476	242
	5,427	2,732	8,426
Increase (decrease) in current liabilities:			
Notes payable	(130)	212	129
Accounts payable	(476)	323	42
Accrued payroll and payroll-related	277	145	9
Profitsharing retirement plan	104	107	9
Accrued income taxes	489	129	9
Deferred Income—Preventive Maintenance Contracts	94	48	20
Other accruals	246	335	(15
	604	1,299	89
Increase in working capital	$4,823	$1,433	$7,52

Figure 9–2.

Note that the sharply rising temporary cash investment reflects but does not equal the difference between the new equity investment and the working capital financing requirement. Other sources may contribute to that difference. Also note that new short-term credit was essentially counterbalanced by a reduction in long-term loans.

Midway Airlines shows a different financial status for its conversion activities (see Figure 9–3). Its first full year of operations in 1980 was characterized by substantial accounting losses from operations of $4.9 million on sales revenue of $24.8 million. The company was establishing new flight routes and airport facilities. It was investing in the conversion capacity represented by long-life assets of airplanes and facilities to serve the future customers. A substantial amount of funds that financed these assets came from external sources of long-term creditors and the sale of common stock to the public. In the subsequent year, with more routes established and planes in operation, sales of $79 million produced a surplus (earnings) of $4.4 million after taxes before *extraordinary* tax credits which allowed for the recoupment of past losses from current tax payments. Even with the net income from operations, the *recoupment of past losses* plus depreciation, all totaling almost $11 million in sources of funds, the company still needed a substantial injection of additional funds to finance its acquisition of more planes and facilities totaling over $32 million during that same year. A reader notes the sharp rise in the short-term investments (marketable securities) component of the working capital breakdown. This comes from the temporary use of cash generated from additional long-term financing and will most likely be spent on the new purchases of long-life assets and possibly for the repayment in the subsequent accounting year of the current maturities of long-term debt which has increased sharply.

When a company is having a difficult time meeting its debt obligations because sales are declining and producing losses, an ultimate major source of funds is available from the liquidation of the production facilities or other long-life assets of the enterprise. Since the current assets are usually financed by current liabilities, their conversion may provide minimal funds. Losses are made up by draining the owners' accumulated retained earnings and paid-in capital. Thus, after Pan American Airlines was having sustained and serious financial difficulties in 1981, it sold its Pan Am office building in New York City

Midway Airlines, Inc.   **Statement of Changes in Financial Position**

	Year ended Dec. 31, 1981	Year ended Dec. 31, 1980	Two-month period ended Dec. 31, 1979
Sources of working capital:			
Operations –			
Income (loss) before extraordinary credit	$ 4,395,771	(4,923,900)	(1,368,904)
Charges not involving working capital:			
Depreciation and amortization –			
Equipment and leasehold improvements	2,712,642	514,401	42,292
Deferred preoperating route extension and other costs	766,081	573,599	82,492
Deferred lease obligations	64,528	476,764	64,524
Deferred income taxes	500,000		
Total provided by (used in) operations before extraordinary credit	8,439,022	(3,359,136)	(1,179,596)
Extraordinary credit	3,162,000		
Total provided by (used in) operations	11,601,022	(3,359,136)	(1,179,596)
Issuance of convertible subordinated notes		6,000,000	
Issuance of long-term notes payable	25,175,224	4,340,525	
Reclassification of notes payable for aircraft purchase deposit		2,562,780	
Application of leased aircraft deposits		326,556	
Net proceeds from public sale of common stock	6,178,255	10,138,391	
Other	141,509	74,252	87,885
Total sources of working capital	43,096,010	20,083,368	(1,091,711)
Uses of working capital:			
Additions to equipment, leasehold improvements and deposits – net	32,161,787	11,940,919	255,374
Reduction in long-term notes payable	5,535,429	903,698	
Additions to deferred preoperating and route extension costs	1,099,653	1,070,574	
Capitalized interest on deposits on aircraft purchases	429,907	421,938	82,736
Increase in other assets	394,435	433,053	45,000
Total uses of working capital	39,621,211	14,770,182	383,110
Increase (decrease) in working capital	$ 3,474,799	5,313,186	(1,474,821)
Changes in elements of working capital:			
Increase (decrease) in current assets –			
Cash	$ 797,309	(77,894)	191,926
Short-term investments	9,090,829	4,494,620	(979,620)
Accounts receivable – net	2,813,285	2,870,024	522,502
Inventories of spare parts and supplies	350,589	(25,792)	325,735
Prepaid expenses	(91,227)	374,763	(11,404)
	12,960,785	7,635,721	49,139
Decrease (increase) in current liabilities –			
Notes payable		2,562,780	
Accounts payable	(1,409,131)	(1,778,697)	(1,019,794)
Air traffic liability	(1,485,925)	(769,058)	(170,401)
Accrued expenses	(2,173,273)	(1,479,212)	(333,765)
Current maturities of long-term notes payable	(4,417,657)	(858,348)	
	(9,485,986)	(2,322,535)	(1,523,960)
Increase (decrease) in working capital	$ 3,474,799	5,313,186	(1,474,821)

Figure 9–3.

and its Intercontinental Hotel chain subsidiary to generate funds in order to avoid default on loans which financed its airline business.

To focus on the use of funds for capital expenditures (long-life assets) is to focus on the capacity of the enterprise to produce *future* surplus. This is clearly evident in the statement of the Midway operations whose business is expanding rapidly. The internal generation of cash from the conversion cycle is far outstripped by the costs of acquiring productive facilities – airplanes. Funds must be raised in the capital markets. Many rapidly growing companies that produce above average surpluses, such as those found in the computer field, have financed their expansions internally from both profits and depreciation flows. Additional financing for production and sales have come from suppliers and commercial banks, whose major role typically consists of the financing of accounts receivable expansion to support growing sales.

As companies reach a point where their rate of capital asset expansion and sales growth slows down, characterized as *mature* companies, use of generated surpluses is increasingly directed toward rewarding investors through dividend payments. In that circumstance, the financing requirement to support the capital asset expansion of a company does not press the cash flow generated from operations. Internal sources of funds generated are often greater than the financing needs of the company. When there is a major new phase of expansion or replacement of production facilities, such large profitable companies with reasonably predictable conversion cycles, and strong balance sheets, usually have better access to external funds than newer companies. Their ability to pay and maintain dividends is in fact an important factor in attracting equity capital.

Projecting external financing needs is part of the business and financial planning of any enterprise. Given sales projections, resource needs can and have to be projected. Cash flow from operations can also be estimated to help determine the external financing requirements. The format of the source and use of funds statement provides managers with a financial planning tool that is particularly effective for growing companies or those in which their conversion cycles are changing significantly or their financing is being reorganized. It focuses on the cash flow from operations, the major source of long-term financing for capacity-building assets. This is the riskier area of asset use and financing in terms of investors' concerns about less established companies since the conversion of these resources is over time and relatively unpredictable. Requirements for additional inventory and accounts receivable financing that also expand with sales are the province of short-term creditors financing the operating cycle, the relatively less risky component of the resource conversion activities.

Part III
Financial Analysis of
Accounting Statements

10
THE OVERVIEW OF THE INVESTORS AND MANAGERS

Investors and managers see different worlds in the same conversion cycle. On one hand, the managers are constantly dealing with a picture of cash flow. They manage funds (cash and credit) flowing from sales to meet the payroll and to purchase other resources. They live in the time frame of cash flow transactions. The income statement tells them, as it tells the financing sources, that sales during a specific period of time were or were not profitable. The information used is extrapolated from past transactions.

Cost calculation methods reflect different attempts by accountants to apportion specific asset use to a unit of sales. They may be fragile matters such as accounting for expenditures that were made more than a decade ago, accounting for current changes in inventory costs or accounting for some recognition that there will most likely be some additional costs incurred in the future for what is sold now. Furthermore, the accounting method is highly influenced by the way in which taxable income is determined by purposes of the state and federal governments. Indeed, the underlying decisions about investment in many conversion cycles are often influenced by government tax policy which encourages and promotes particular types of investment with tax incentives. Good examples are low income housing, solar energy, research and development, and export sales.

Because income statements are extrapolations and apportionments of costs of resources used in a time period, the balance sheet shows residuals of those assets which remain to be sold. Yet, we don't think of productive facilities being *sold* so much as being used up. The accountant's views of using a long-life asset are based on formulas for depreciation. These are accounting constructions and rationales; they may have little to do with actual use, durability, and obsolescence. Indeed, these calculations are also very much related to the tax policy and procedures for measuring the cost of using long-life assets. Above all, the accounting is focused on past transactions. Valuation of assets is mainly established by their acquisition costs. Expected value of available assets in the marketplace is something which will only be revealed in future sales. Expected obligations from the financing of the conversion cycle, however, are predictable and accountable.

Regardless of the shortcomings and questioning of accounting methodology, it offers a systematic approach to financial measurement of past business decisions. Results of a conversion cycle for any given time are measured in the income statement. The balance sheet shows the flow of resources used up and acquired along with changes in the financing and financial commitments. These documents are summary statements categorizing many individual transactions. Behind each number within each category lies a compilation of transactions. Part of the job of the accountant involves segregating flows of transactions in order to compile accurate records. Accountants are in the financial information systems business. This information is used by managers to track and control costs and to measure uses and flows of resources in the conversion cycle.

Ultimately investors look at the questions of getting their money back and getting some reward for the use of it. For lenders, the interest rate is the return on their investment. They take a limited risk in the cycle and derive a limited return. They usually have a specifically contracted time frame for the use of their money. This time frame often correlates with the expected conversion of individual resources or groups of resources. The level of their reward or return, the interest rates for their money, usually depends on two factors: (1) the general supply and demand conditions for borrowed funds and (2) the individual risk factors of the conversion cycle of a particular enterprise. The former is determined by the monetary policy of the banking system and changing macro-economic conditions. The latter is a matter of many conditions pertaining to the loan contract as well as the particular business outlook (risk of the conversion cycle) and resource use of the particular enterprise.

For owners, investing their money means the possible generation of surpluses from undertaking the conversion cycle. Those earnings can be very substantial or very small. There are no limitations to investment returns, except on preferred shares. If the conversion activities don't work out, owners' investment is lost. Only five out of 100 new businesses last more than 10 years. Nevertheless, the fountain of new products and services flows from new business ventures. One need only look at the computer industry to sense the entrepreneurial spirit. The undertaking of a business conversion, whether it is a new restaurant or a multimillion dollar shopping center, bears the same risk elements for investors, regardless of amounts of money involved.

BREAKING EVEN

A single basic analytical framework exists for the operation and development of the conversion cycle and understanding how its surpluses are generated. It is called *breakeven analysis.* The fundamental idea is that a certain level of resources are needed to run a business regardless of the level of sales that are generated within any given time period. They represent the available capacity, and their costs do not change very much with volume of output, unless the capacity changes. Other costs of resource use vary directly with sales volume. The sale of milk from a refrigerator offers a simplified example. The actual number of quarts of milk sold may vary over any specific time period, but the costs of having the capacity of the refrigerator available are more or less fixed – space rent, maintenance, electricity, depreciation. Breakeven analysis considers the difference between the price received and the direct or wholesale cost of a unit (quart of milk) and the sales volume needed which will provide enough money to cover the ongoing, relatively unchanging or fixed costs related to the refrigeration capacity. The volume of sales which will cover all costs of producing those sales is the breakeven volume, measured in units or sales dollars. At higher volumes, profits will expand until operational capacity is reached. At lower volumes, losses will be incurred, since total revenues from sales will not have covered the total costs to produce those sales.

ASSET TURNOVER

Closely related to this operational framework is the rapidity of the cycle of conversion of the resources employed. The particular financial reference to this aspect of conversion is *asset turnover*. It offers a guideline to the amount of financing required for an enterprise. In the case of the sale of milk from a refrigeration machine, the stored volume may be sold within a few days. The cash-to-milk-to-sale-to-cash cycle, the financing time, is short. The resource turns into cash rapidly; the same cash is reinvested to replace the milk sold. That level of cash can produce a large volume of annual sales depending on the rapidity of the resource turnover. But if you built harps, four per year, the turnover of the output from cash-to-resources (raw materials and labor) to the finished harp-to-sale-to-cash would take three months. Cash would be tied up for a relatively long time. Yet both activities could have the same breakeven sales level of surplus. Most important though is that very different amounts of financing are required for differing lengths of time in the conversion of the assets.

Each time a unit of output is sold, a *contribution* (the difference between the price received and the wholesale or manufactured cost) is made to recouping the fixed costs of capacity. So the volume of sales in any given time frame is based upon conversion of saleable assets, and that in turn is directly related to financing levels. If sales are made on credit rather than for cash, then the conversion to cash is slower. The credit given to the buyer has to be financed by the enterprise. The longer the conversion time, the greater the cost to make the sale, often explicitly accounted for by the cost of commercial bank loans.

RATIO ANALYSIS

Ratio analysis is a way of comparing different components of the financial information compiled about the conversion activities. Ratios are used to compare the periodic changes in the cost of resource components used up in the sales in a particular enterprise or to compare with similar information about any industry. The ratios relate surplus generated with assets employed and financing levels. Ratios provide a relative measure of changes in the financial measures of (1) profitability, (2) efficient use of assets, (3) the ability to pay current liabilities, and (4) the ability to meet long-term and fixed obligations. Thus, managers, creditors, and owners typically use

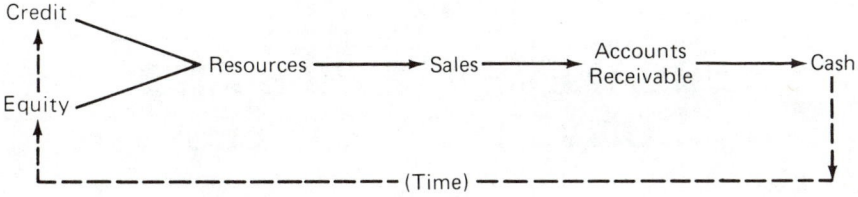

Figure 10-1.

these measurements to consider cost controls, to estimate financial flows and earnings, and to check the safety of invested capital.

These measurements are abstracted from the conversion cycle. The information is taken from the income statement and balance sheet formats as seen in Figure 10–1. The measurements emphasize:

1. Time that investors moneys are involved in the cycle.
2. Changes in cost of producing sales and returns to owners for the use of their capital.
3. Sales in relation to resources employed.
4. The effect of using debt on both earnings and cash flow.

All earnings of (returns to) investors are relative. The accounting time of one year is standard in order to make comparisons. (Certainly they can be calculated on a daily or monthly basis.) The returns, or losses, in a large part result from decisions made by managers of the conversion cycle. The measurement of the results is also a matter of accounting procedures and current taxation policies. For example, if the rate of corporate income tax is lowered, the net income after tax will increase owing to no effort on the part of the managers/decisionmakers. Owners' investment will show a higher return of surplus in relation to the same amount of assets employed in the conversion cycle. The risks of the cycle will not have changed. Furthermore, if the general income tax laws change, then comparisons with other businesses and industries will reflect the same change. Part of the financial analyst's job is to separate and clarify the difference between the risks of the conversion cycle itself and the application of the measuring factors.

11
BREAKEVEN LEVELS AND CONVERSION CYCLES

BREAKEVEN ANALYSIS

The profit and loss statement shows a formal recognition of two categories of costs:

1. Those which vary directly with the volume of sales.
2. Those which are indirect and are required to operate the capacity of the enterprise regardless of the level of sales.

This division of costs of resources used and financing essentially reflects the difference between costs incurred in the conversion that cannot be associated with a particular volume of sales and those directly related to specific sales. If long-term debt financing is used, then the cost of such financing (interest) is also considered as a part of the capacity cost, but it is separated to show that it derives from the financing arrangement rather than from asset use.

Indirect or fixed costs incurred during a sales period include the costs of buildings, machinery and equipment, rent, and the costs of organizing operations with specialized skills such as administration, sales, promotion, engineering, warehouse management, bookkeeping, and more. The particular composition depends on the nature of the resources used in the conversion cycle and how they are financed. These costs, as noted earlier, represent in the general sense the production capacity. They are separated from the direct costs of materials, skills, energy and other resource costs directly associated with the particular units sold. Many examples of both (1) long-life and (2) short-life resources have been given throughout this book:

Farm production requires: (1) farm land, machinery and a manager/ farmer, (2) seeds, fertilizer, farm labor

Dental services requires: (1) office space, dental equipment, office furniture and equipment, and secretarial staff, (2) dentist's labor and supplies

Grocery business requires: (1) store space, refrigeration and display equipment, advertising, cashiers, and stock people, (2) stock of goods on the shelves

Consider the effects of unit costs of sales as production expands in the conversion cycle. The direct costs increase proportionate to sales while the fixed costs for the level of capacity and financing fall on a per unit basis. Stating the effect of expanding conversion cycles differently: as volume increases, unit costs (total costs ÷ number of units), whether they are for bushels of wheat or total hours of dental services, contain proportionately less fixed costs. Because the manager's or secretary's salary, depreciation level, rent, and other fixed costs are divided by the total output, these components of the total cost of each unit declines. The total cost per unit falls *until* capacity of a given amount of managerial, technical, physical resources, and financing is reached. That level of operation marks an ideal volume of a conversion cycle since it maximizes the utilization of the resources employed in the conversion activity. (See Figure 11–1.)

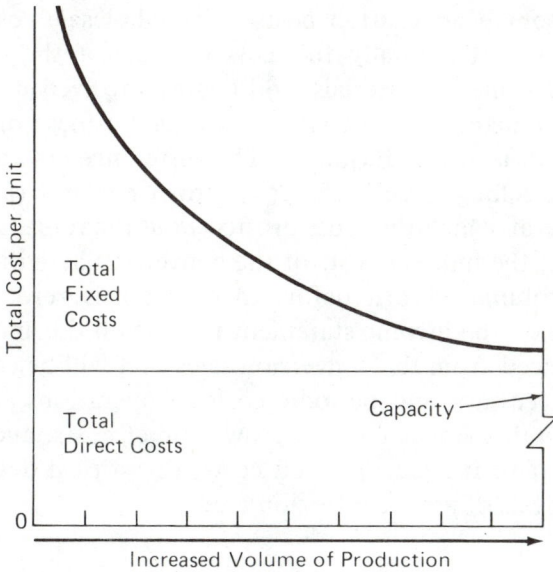

Figure 11–1.

The concept of breakeven says that when a certain volume of sales is achieved (at a given price per unit), all costs of producing it will be returned to the conversion cycle.

Sales (price × number of units) = Cost of Goods Sold
(direct cost/unit × number of units)

+ Operating and Financial Costs (Indirect)

Beyond that volume, only direct costs will continue to be incurred proportionate to sales. The indirect or fixed costs of the resources employed for capacity of the conversion cycle will have been recouped. Therefore, surplus will be generated with increased sales. The division of the direct and indirect costs on the income statement holds the key to the pricing and volume level that the conversion activities require.

The difference between the price and the wholesale cost of the milk (the costs of the goods sold) is commonly referred to as the *mark-up*. It reflects the percentage that the selling price is raised over the resource acquisition costs. The wholesale cost in retailing forms its basis. Essentially this cost consists of the cost of labor, factory management, materials, and energy involved in the unit production in a manufacturing or processing business or the cost of direct labor in a service business. The difference between the direct cost and the selling price is the gross profit per unit (page 82). The sales volume at which the gross profits *equal* the remainder of the incurred costs, the indirect costs of the conversion activities, marks the breakeven volume. Profit before income tax is zero. Accounting information on the income statement focuses on the amount of gross profit produced from the conversion sales that will be contributed to cover the necessary and periodic costs of operations and financing. Since each unit of sales covers its own direct costs, and contributes some amount to indirect or fixed costs, the critical determinants of breakeven levels of asset conversion are:

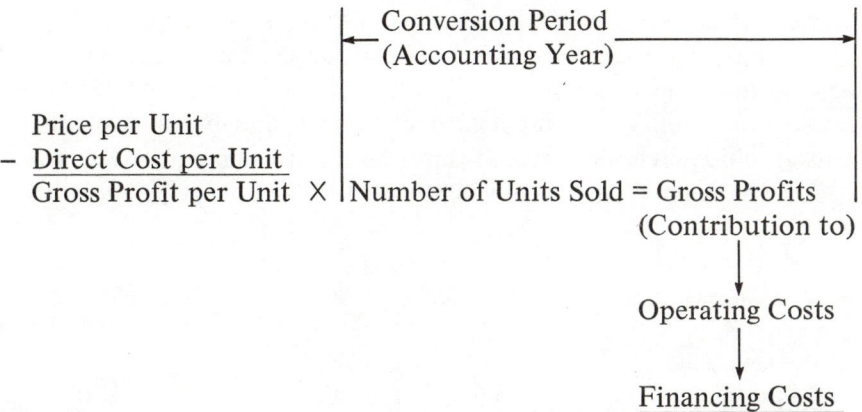

The assets conversion shown above produces for the owners either (1) a loss, (2) 0 (breakeven), or (3) a surplus. At the point where the indirect costs are fully covered, there is no loss nor surplus from the conversion. It marks the sales volume where all costs of production have been recouped. Therefore, the owners are not losing their money during that period of sales. Increased sales only require additional direct costs, as long as there is available

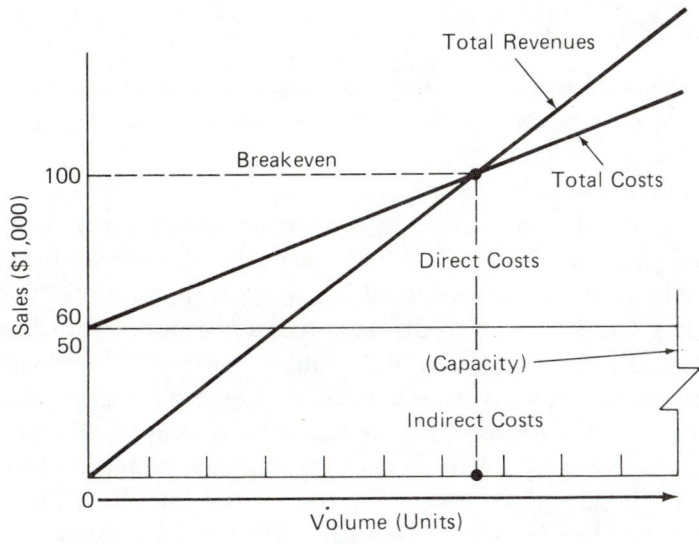

Figure 11–2.

productive capacity of the fixed cost resources. Graphically, Figure 11–2 shows the relationship between costs, sales revenues, and volume in its most simplified version as commonly given in lectures, texts, and seminars on financial management and business planning. This graphic perception, which is not conversion-time oriented, translates into a time frame income statement in the following accounting format.

Sales per year	$80,000	$100,000	$110,000	$120,000
Units (Price = $10/unit)	(8,000)	(10,000)	(11,000)	(12,000)
Cost of Goods Sold				
($4 per unit)	$32,000	$ 40,000	$ 44,000	$ 48,000
Gross Profits	48,000	60,000	66,000	72,000
Operating Costs	50,000	50,000	50,000	50,000
Financing Costs	10,000	10,000	10,000	10,000
(Total cost per unit sold)	($11.50)	($10.00)	($9.45)	($9.00)
Earnings Before Taxes	($12,000)	0 ·	$6,000	$ 12,000

Accounting effects on the conversion cycle (as measured on the balance sheet)

Owners' capital	(–12,000)	no change	surplus added

The surplus added to the owners' capital is essentially the gross profit from each additional sale *after* the breakeven level, less the income tax levy.

If an enterprise always operates above the breakeven level in its resource conversion activities then it will always show a surplus. But many businesses typically do not operate above breakeven volume all the time. Commercial activities such as tourist facilities operate at very high levels of utilization and profitability during their season while losing money out of season. Department stores generally lose money in February/March and July/August, and for most of them, the major part of their profitability is generated from sales in December. Since certain costs are incurred year round, a minimum level of sales that produces gross profits will contribute something to cover these costs. Seasonally affected businesses are often run at a loss during the off season only to be made up at a different point in the conversion cycle, i.e., gross profits are more or less than the fixed costs at different levels of capacity within the conversion cycle as measured annually.

When new businesses are organized and begin to sell their products and services, they lose money. Midway Airlines lost money in its first full year of operations and generated considerable surplus in its second year when passenger volume surpassed breakeven level through rapidly expanding sales. Furthermore, operations were profitable even though breakeven levels increased, reflecting significantly expanded operational costs due to the purchases of additional airplanes and the establishment of new routes.

Actual volume of sales is accounted for in the time frame of the income statement. But on the basis of a continuous conversion cycle, a certain production capacity of an enterprise must be utilized in order to recoup continuous periodic costs. When capacity expands, indirect costs will be higher and breakeven volume will increase if prices charged and direct costs have not changed. Many a small restaurant has found itself in financial hot water when success has led to a too rapid expansion of dining facilities. Rental costs usually increase sharply along with payments to the bank that financed the remodeling and increased seating capacity. Monthly cash outflow swells. Sales volume increases, but added gross profits are not enough to cover increased operating costs.

Breakeven is price sensitive. The idea of passing along increased labor costs, for example, means maintaining the same gross profit per unit or dollar of sales. Hopefully, buyers are willing to and can pay more for the same product or service. But if direct costs cannot be passed along to the buyer, then the gross profit per unit of sales declines and the breakeven sales volume will increase. When competition limits price increases or forces price reductions as in the airline and personal computer industries, profit margins shrink. Unless sales volume is expanded, gross profits fall. In industries like computers and calculators, sales volume has sharply increased in response to price reduction. On the other hand, De Beers, the diamond producer that controls 80% of the international marketing of diamonds, keeps prices from falling, thus maintaining profits, by limiting supplies available to buyers. Insofar as a new enterprise has a product that is needed and does not have much competition, its managers often seek the price of what the market will bear. The gross margins are as high as they can possibly be. Prices eventually come down with competition and if volume expands, gross profits increase in spite of limitations on the price.

There are many factors that affect changes in the cost of components resources use, pricing of the output, and volume of sales. These comprise the management challenge and the investors' risk of the conversion cycle as discussed in earlier chapters. One of the more important financial translations of the breakeven perspective came with the deregulation of the airline industry which began in 1978. When ticket prices became subject to competitive influences they fell. Lower prices were expected to produce increased volume, which they did. However, fuel oil, a major direct cost, more than doubled in 1980, sharply squeezing gross profit margins even further. Interest rates rose steadily and wages rose in the inflationary economy. Airline traffic started sliding with the economic downturn that followed. To add to the picture, small airline companies started to spring up, buying used, therefore heavily depreciated, aircraft and hiring on a nonunion basis. The latter became more feasible as layoffs in the industry and general unemployment increased. The smaller, no-frills airlines had lower fixed as well as direct costs in getting their planes off the ground. They were particularly profitable in the shorter flights where large airlines are often high-cost operators. By 1983, much lower long-term interest rates had evolved while lower fuel prices had prevailed and an economic upturn started. All these influences shifted the breakeven calculations and profitability of different flights, planes, and companies.

The core of the breakeven analysis is the interrelationship between ongoing indirect costs and the variable costs, the pricing and quantity of units sold. Since indirect costs represent a level of capacity of the equipment facilities and management skills; the more units sold, the greater the resource utilization and the lower the total unit cost to produce them. Hence the greater the profitability per unit of sales, assuming the selling price and the direct costs do not change. This occurs because the indirect costs such as the president's salary, the annual advertising expenditures, the annual accounting fees, the receptionist's salary and other regularly incurred costs are divided by a greater number of units as sales increase. The limit of the sales volume is the capacity, which is reflected in the fixed costs. Production or wholesale costs generally vary directly and proportionately to the price and the volume. The calculation of unit costs is illustrated in the following table:

Number of Units Sold	Indirect (Fixed) Costs (annualized)	Direct (Variable) Costs ($4/unit)	Total Cost	Unit Cost
5,000	$70,000	$ 20,000	$ 90,000	$18.00
10,000	$70,000	$ 40,000	$110,000	$11.00
15,000	$70,000	$ 60,000	$130,000	$ 8.67
20,000	$70,000	$ 80,000	$150,000	$ 7.50
30,000 (full capacity)	$70,000	$120,000	$190,000	$ 6.33

If the market price for the product was $10.50, the contribution margin of each unit of sales would be the price less the direct cost, which equals $6.50. Therefore, breakeven volume would be equal to $70,000 ÷ $6.50 or 10,770 units. The company must be assured that it can sell this level of output in one year in order to return the costs incurred for the resources employed in one year.

If the price falls or if it is reduced for volume sales discounts or if wages and materials costs increase, the contribution of gross profits to cover fixed costs falls. If the managers take a pay cut or if the advertising budget is reduced or if the interest rate on borrowed money falls, the fixed costs fall. The breakeven level declines as a result of reductions in fixed costs. If the same company expands its production capacity, the fixed costs rise substantially, initially increasing the unit costs until the new facilities are more fully utilized.

Number of Units Sold	Expansion Fixed Costs (annual)	Variable Costs ($4.00/unit)	Total Cost	Unit Cost
30,000	$90,000	$120,000	$210,000	$7.00
40,000	$90,000	$160,000	$250,000	$6.25
50,000	$90,000	$200,000	$290,000	$5.80
60,000 (full capacity)	$90,000	$240,000	$330,000	$5.50

In the real world, resource costs change, and more efficient configurations of resource uses are developed. Cost-volume-profit analysis in an ongoing enterprise would consider the effects of a range of variable cost possibilities along with a range of price and volume considerations. The management practices and decision making about quantity sales discounting, high level production runs, multishift use of production equipment, and variable pricing based on slightly different product models can all be explained through an elaboration and manipulation of the relationships between indirect costs, sales prices, and volume. The greater the utilization of capacity, the lower the unit cost of sales. However, where new products require significant product development and introduction costs, higher levels of indirect costs are involved. They may require high prices for recuperation of such expenditures. As those one-time cost outlays are recovered, the remaining components of indirect unit costs fall. Thus, if competition is also increasing, prices have to be reduced, though the contribution margins will fall. Adding a related product to an ongoing and profitable business essentially means risking only the direct costs of the product, since most indirect costs are already being recouped. The same salespeople can sell 12 products instead of 10. Gross profit margins generated from additional new product sales after breakeven level has been reached may be for all practical purposes substantially equal to additional profit before taxes.

The book publishing business provides a good example of risk taking with new products. An additional new book contracted for publication requires input from the publisher's staff (indirect costs) who are paid for their skills of editing, marketing, publicity, bookkeeping, and more. These are fixed costs representing a certain level of capacity of book development. They are paid out of ongoing sales. For the book itself, a substantial part of the resources cost involved is provided by the author. The manuscript, the raw product, is usually acquired by the publisher from the author on a purely speculative basis of payment. That payment for the idea and writing skill is a *royalty,* a predetermined percentage of the sale price of the book received by the publisher. Payment is based on future sales. An advance against future royalties is often part of a publisher's contract with an author. It is a direct cost to the publisher, usually expected to be recouped from the sale of the first printing. The publisher risks additional direct costs of printing the prepared manuscript and possibly advertising costs for each new book. Thus, the main costs of the publisher in assuming the production and sale of a new work consist primarily of these limited direct costs.

As the new book is sold, the direct costs are recouped, along with initial promotion costs. There are little if any additional fixed costs for the additional book. Thus, at any given time in the conversion cycle, the publisher's risk is primarily the production cost of the unsold books and the balance of the unrecouped advanced royalty. The reward is essentially the gross profit on each sale. One successful book can shoulder the risk of conversion of numerous books. At risk to the author is the value of his or her resource input, solely determined by future sales. Unfortunately, most books produce relatively little financial return to their authors in terms of the time and mental efforts expended to write them. Where a manuscript is sold outright to publishers with no royalty arrangements, the author is paid for his or her skills. The publisher acquires a long-life amortizable resource and takes the full risk of financing the resource costs of producing and selling a book.

Where resource suppliers share the risk of conversion by financing direct costs, as with authors and artists selling on consignment, the acquiring enterprise needs less investment in its saleable inventory. The conversion revenues however must provide adequate gross profits to cover the normal periodic operating costs. There is no change in the breakeven analysis, only a change or shift in the parties bearing the risk.

FINANCIAL LEVERAGE – THE RISKS AND BENEFITS OF BORROWING

Insofar as resources are financed by creditors, payments of annual interest charges become a part of the indirect costs of operating a business. For the overall conversion, they become a fixed part of the outflow of cash and are treated separately on the income statement. Repayments of the principal of a loan are not costs but return of financing, therefore, a reduction in resources. They are however an intricate part of the cash flow pattern of the conversion cycle. Interest costs are calculated on a periodic basis. Those pertaining to long-life asset financing do not relate to specific levels of production, only to the availability of specific assets. (Interest costs related to financing current assets expand and contract with the volume of these assets.) As more credit is employed to finance long-life resources, the level of interest costs forces upward the break-even volume necessary to cover all costs of conversion. Companies with major capital assets such as hotels, airplanes, or pipelines typically use a high level of long-term debt relative to total financing as part of their financial structure. Consequently, a significant part of their annual revenues go to meeting the annual interest costs that compose a large part of their total costs of the conversion cycle. Loan repayments also make up a significant cash outflow of their conversion cycles. The direct costs of filling another seat in the airplane or putting another occupant in the hotel rooms is very small relative to the price received for the services. Thus, in such conversions where the key resources of the business activity are expensive long-life capital assets, the gross margin or gross profit per unit is very high. Operating costs over a wide range of asset utilization do not change — the number of people at the 16-hour reservation desks, the number of seats or rooms in the planes and hotels, the levels of annual interest charges, depreciation, etc. Once these costs have been recouped at the breakeven sales levels, the surplus thereafter expands rapidly as sales increases.

If owners invested only their money in long-life resources, the surplus generated from the conversion cycle would be a return on their investment alone. By using creditors' funds, they *leverage* this return. They gain from the use of creditor financing of resources employed as long as the surplus generated from those additional resources in use is greater than the added cost of the credit. The owners' investment may be only a fraction of the total cost of the assets employed (balance sheet) yet they receive the total surplus (operating profits) from the conversion cycle less the interest cost paid to the lenders/investors. Since the cost of long-term debt is generally a fixed percentage of the loan funds borrowed, it does not change with resource utilization, and the generation of gross profits. (Short-term financing, being directly related to the expansion and contraction of the current assets of inventory and accounts receivable is effectively a direct cost of sales.) The annual depreciation cost does not change in relation to sales regardless of whether the asset is financed by owners or creditors. The income statement format separates the asset use (operating) costs from the financial (leverage) costs where it shows Earning Before Interest and Taxes (EBIT). This value in any given time period equals the sales less the total cost of the resources used to produce them. Insofar as these earnings (operating profits) equal interest costs, operations are at the breakeven level, which incorporates financing costs.

Adding major resource capacity (capital equipment) requires generating enough use to cover its costs of additional management (if any) and depreciation. The same assets, when financed through debt rather than through owners' equity, cause the breakeven level of operations to be higher. Therefore the risk of conversion increases; because when debt is employed to finance it, a substantial added cost of conversion must be recouped in its use. As debt is repaid, the annual interest cost falls. Furthermore in a cash flow sense, the use of debt also increases the level of repayment obligations (in addition to interest) that must be recovered from the cash generated from the conversion cycle.

As Midway Airlines expanded its airplane fleet and facilities with debt financing, its interest charges rose from $600,000 to $2 million by its second full year of passenger operations. With sales rising very rapidly, this indirect cost was easily absorbed by rapidly increasing gross profits. The owners' investment was enhanced by added surplus. Unfortunately for Braniff Airlines, their expansion did not generate the passenger revenues and gross profits to pay for its expansion costs. Profit margins per passenger revenue mile fell sharply because of competitive discount pricing of air fares and the dramatic increase in fuel costs, a major direct cost of producing passenger seat miles. Operating profits were inadequate to cover financing charges. Cash outflow from losses drained the company's equity.

In sum, expensive long-life assets are usually leveraged through debt financing. As long as their utilization is great enough to pay for the interest and related operational costs, as well as to generate enough cash through depreciation flow to repay loans, then the risk of their use is covered. However, a conversion cycle may last many years, so risks of income generation and cash flow depend on asset utilization *and* a time frame much greater than the yearly accounting cycle.

VARIATIONS ON THE BREAKEVEN THEME

Profitability or the generation of surplus from the conversion cycle in any given time frame depends on the interaction of the (1) selling price or prices, (2) the volume of sales, (3) the variable cost per unit and the fixed costs of the organizational capacity, and (4) the product mix being sold. The various combinations will produce differing results. A story in the *Wall Street Journal* (5/12/81) about Philips Industries is illustrative of a management's response to the effects of recession on the company's operations. During the increasingly difficult economic times of 1979 and 1982, a steady reduction of sales produced an *increase* in profits! No accounting wizardry was involved. Their overall strategy was to change markets but not product lines and reduce administrative overhead, their operating cost levels. The company's products were for the housing market which constricted dramatically in those years as interest rates rose. Management took action initially to eliminate products which generated low profit margins — commodity-type sales, easily made by other companies. In place of these highly competitive, low-margin products, some product lines were upgraded. Their production required greater technology but generated much higher gross profit margins. In one decision they started selling directly to dealers instead of through wholesalers, thereby expanding gross profit margins significantly while only expanding marketing (indirect) costs slightly. They also reduced administrative costs, closed and consolidated some of their manufacturing facilities, and rearranged their trucking activities. Thus falling indirect costs reflected the decline in the levels of assets needed in the conversion cycle. Volume of sales fell, but profits rose because of expanded margins on higher priced items and reduced operating costs. They continued to make most of the same product lines but upgraded them or sought different markets. For example with excess axle-making capacity previously used for production and sales to the recreation vehicle industry, they sought new markets for this component in agriculture and other nonrecreational trailer businesses.

Business decisions always involve a combination of cost factors, risks of not producing sales, and pricing flexibility. The importance of breakeven analysis is the construction of a framework for weighing cost variables and changes in sales levels to determine alternative choices in terms of their resource inputs and profitability outcomes. A matrix that shows a variation in prices per unit, direct unit costs, and fixed costs, along with volume changes will produce a combination of profitability alternatives and returns to the equity investors. Computer business programs are designed for this type of comparison of financial data and calculations. The effects of "What if" iterations can be immediately and easily calculated for those who are making decisions about acquiring resources and pricing their output.

BREAKEVEN – ACCOUNTING CALCULATION OR CASH FLOW EXPERIENCE?

Up to this point, the concept of breakeven has been mainly explored in terms of the accounting view extrapolated from the income statement. Accounting breakeven means to reach the level of sales where the total costs equals the total revenues. It does not contain a time frame of the actual inflow of revenues and outflow of expenditures. Indirect (operating and financing) costs which must be recouped consist of a combination of periodic outlays, a large portion of which may be salaries for administrative and technical people as well as noncash charges of depreciation or amortization and interest. From the managerial point of view, cash flowing out of the enterprise goes to the regular acquisition and replacement salaries, other operating expenses, payments of interest and principal of loans. It does not include the cost of using up long-life assets. Thus, in the short run, breakeven for the manager means to reach the point where gross profits cover repetitive indirect costs exclusive of noncash charges such as depreciation and amortization. In an accounting sense, operations are running at a loss, all accounting costs are not being recouped. From a cash flow sense, the recoupment of long-life asset costs are being delayed. There is no current cash drain if they were bought with owners' cash. However, if the enterprise financed long-life asset acquisition through loans, then cash recoupment must be great enough to cover the loan repayments. An accounting loss

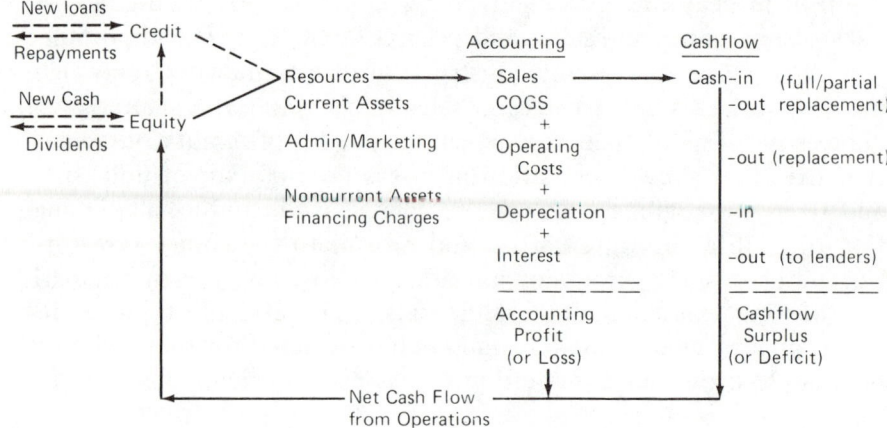

Figure 11–3.

may still be shown. (See Figure 11–3.) Depreciation, as a noncash cost or accounting charge, is in effect a periodic recoupment of an original investment in long-life resources financed by either borrowed funds or owners' capital. As long as operations are at accounting breakeven, it is a source of funds that can be used for resource replacement and addition, repayment of loans, or returned to owners.

Commercial real estate can be operated at an accounting loss to the benefit of the owners as long as rental income covers maintenance costs, rental services, and loan repayments, the major sources of cash outflow. At accounting breakeven, depreciation often provides more cash than loan repayments, thus owners gain by a return of their original investment. If a loan covered 80% of the purchase price of a building, the loan's funds in effect "bought" 80% of the flow of depreciation (recoupment) for the owners. They can show an accounting loss from their operations yet have a cash distribution from the depreciation charge against annual income.

With accelerated depreciation, earlier life-cycle cash recoupment from using long-life equipment may be considerably higher than loan repayment levels. Enterprises and individuals whose business is renting long-life assets financed with a high proportion of debt can often generate cash flow and accounting losses to be used as a tax offset to profitable conversion activity or as tax deductible "write-offs" for themselves.

Some investors may have been very pleased to have owned oil drilling rigs during 1981, when rental demand for their equipment was at a premium. Initial high levels of accelerated depreciation *sheltered* rental income which was greater than loan repayments, thus providing tax-free income to them. Financial leverage facilitated high returns to investors. A good deal! But they lost their smile by the end of 1982 when drilling activity had dropped to less than half of what it had been a year earlier when oil prices were spiraling. Owners were left with expensive assets financed with large amounts of debt and almost nonexistent demand for drill rigs. Accounting losses mounted and cash flow became negative. Creditors took back the rigs, which were the security for their loans, when owners could not make repayments. Furthermore, like the Braniff creditors, these lenders found that the market values of the partially depreciated assets were well below the remainder of their unrecovered loans because of an oversupply of used rigs for sale.

Investors, both creditors and owners, should be mindful that conversion risks are still the basis for all investment returns and cash flow patterns. If rentals do not cover annual costs plus a scheduled loan repayment then the owners must pay out the differential or be faced with the possibility of losing their property to the creditors. The attraction for private investors in these types of tax-sheltered investments in long-life assets is the high level of depreciation which creates a nontaxable cash flow since it is the return of the cost of the asset. As long as credit is used to purchase the assets, the risk of being unable to repay loans and the added interest costs remains the primary consideration of the investors, rather than the tax value of the accounting losses.

For owners and managers of ongoing businesses, cash is generated from operations through depreciation in addition to the surplus generated over the costs of specific sales. In the immediate managing perspective, current bills have to be paid from revenues generated by sales. In the longer run, all financing has to be returned to investors, both lenders and owners, along with a reward for their risks in financing the conversion cycle.

12
FINANCIAL ANALYSIS

RATIO ANALYSIS

Investors look at their investment in terms of safety and gain. Questions like "How productively are the assets of the company being utilized?" "Is this loan safe?" "Is this company as profitable an investment as another?" represent the three levels of interest of those involved in resource conversion activities. Managers making daily decisions are concerned with developing growing businesses and controlling costs. Lenders look at the flow of resources through the conversion cycle and the way it produces cash to repay their funds as well as to earn interest. Owners look to the generation of surplus as their reward for undertaking the greater level of investors' risk. They look at profitability of sales and growth of their equity as well as at distributions of surplus.

Ratio analysis is a blanket term for the comparison of the relationship of different financial transactions in the ongoing conversion cycle. Managers have a particular interest in the relationship between costs and revenues from sales. Bankers are concerned with the *turnover* (the conversion cycle) of current assets, since they are major financiers of production and sales credit. Bond holders watch the changing levels of funds available from sales to cover the interest costs and contracted annual repayments. Some owners, especially those with income-producing investments, look at dividend payout in relationship to earnings. Others, concerned with risk, look at the amount of debt in the total financing. Most of the ratios are of mutual concern to all the parties involved since they offer ways of measuring performance and risk in the conversion activities. All measurement is relative, either in the historical context of the conversion cycle of an entity or with other entities in the same industry.

Ratio analysis provides financial guidelines to help answer questions about conversion decisions pertaining to profitable use of assets and the risks of financing the cycle. An endless number of ratios can be developed from components of the income statements and balance sheets but there are four key areas that embrace most financial use of ratios. In addition, the financial analyst, when looking at a particular enterprise, concentrates on the types of financial transactions most important to the particular industry. For example, in the electric utility industry, a substantial cost of producing power has to do with the cost of energy (oil, coal) and the cost of the enormous amount of debt financing used to acquire power-generating and distribution facilities. It is a capital-intensive industry whose conversion cycle is mainly based on very large long-life resources. Other businesses, such as construction, employ considerable human resources which may account for a large part of their costs of production. Thus, different industries — service, processing, agriculture, mining, transportation, and so on — have different compositions and flows of resource acquisition, use, and financing patterns. Financial analysis accordingly must weigh and measure the most relevant component transactions.

Operating Ratios and Profitability

From the manager's perspective, everyday decisions are eventually weighed against the *bottom line,* the level of surplus (profitability) that sales produce in any given time frame. The surplus consists of a residual from subtracting the cost of goods or services sold and indirect costs from the prices received for them. As discussed in earlier chapters, accounting methods vary on calculating cost, but with consistency in the use of particular principles, the information can be comparative. Two or more consecutive income statements will enable a periodic comparison of component costs to produce a unit of sales or a sales dollar. Four or five will show a defined trend. The profit margin, the ratio of net income after tax to sales, or net profit per dollar of sales, is the ultimate measure of the profitability of sales. However, each cost component can be measured to determine why the financial margin went up or down. For example, in the cosmetics industry, advertising costs as a percent of the sales dollar are a substantial and critical component of any financial analysis. Cost of new product introductions or an advertising war between companies will have a major impact on earnings per dollar of sales. The results are reflected in changes in the ratios. These changes are financial guides, a signaling system for the financial analyst. By comparing percentages of component costs on the income statement, one can see where shifts are taking place.

The income statement form emphasizes (1) *gross profit margin,* the difference between the direct costs of sales and the selling price, and (2) the *operating profit,* earnings before interest and taxes. These two margins separately reflect changes in the two specific categories of resource use that compose direct and indirect costs. The third profit margin, *earnings before income tax,* takes into account the cost of debt financing in the conversion cycle and nonoperating income and losses from interest earned and extraordinary transactions. At this point in the income statement, all costs incurred to produce sales are recognized. Setting aside the effects of the extraordinary transactions, and temporary interest earnings, the focus is purely on the cost of the conversion cycle and the effect of using debt to finance it. The surplus or loss for the owners is significantly influenced by the debt incurred. The interest cost, therefore, reduces the surplus generated.

The impact of using debt financing is expressed separately from the costs of operation. It relates primarily to the risk of the owners rather than to the costs of production per se. While owners have more resources available to the conversion cycle when debt financing is employed, the breakeven level rises because of financing costs. As long as the operating income generated from the resources financed by debt exceeds the level of interest charges, the equity investors benefit. Even a small addition to surplus may cause a significant rise in the relation of the surplus to the invested equity, since the latter has not increased. The trade-off, however, is that the breakeven level rises with more debt, and the risk of being unable to meet debt repayment obligations also rises.

The best guide to analyzing earnings or surplus generated from the conversion is found in the earnings before income taxes, since taxation of income is external to the conversion cycle and unrelated to it. Payroll or real estate taxes, however, are regular costs of doing business and affect profit margins. A change in the business income tax level, a political action, will only change the *net* profit margin after tax. It has no effect on the costs of producing the sales; they remain the same.

The operating ratios consider costs and profits in relation to sales. They essentially measure the management capability of controlling costs. For the operations of Haemonetics from the beginning of 1980 to the end of 1982, the income statements show the following trends in costs and revenues:

	1979	%	1980	%	1981	%
Sales (1,000)	$19,256		$23,954		$30,013	
COGC	8,833		10,655		14,276	
Gross Profits	10,423	54	12,299	56	15,737	52
Selling, General & Admin.	5,947		7,306		8,591	
Product Development	938		1,196		1,546	
Depreciation	419		569		840	
Operating Income	3,121	16	3,228	13	5,750	19
Interest Expense	(165)		(349)		(415)	
Interest Income	161		323		970	
Other Income (expenses)	59		(49)		(416)	
Income before Taxes	3,174	16.5	4,153	17.3	4,899	16.3
Taxes (rate)	1,477 (46.5)		1,957 (47.1)		2,210 (45.1)	
Net Income	1,697	8.8	2,196	9.2	2,689	9.0

Earnings in relation to the number of common ownership shares are divided by the weighted average number of shares outstanding at the end of the last fiscal period, providing an earnings per share (EPS) figure.

$0.85 $1.01 $1.12

ROI or ROE, the *return on the equity investment,* measures the surplus earned from the conversion cycle in terms of the owners' investment. The ownership reward is the net income after tax in relation to the total owners' investment of paid-in capital and accumulated earnings from the past that have been reinvested in the conversion cycle. Changes in owner financing seriously affect this ratio. In the case of Haemonetics, the ROE in 1980, a year in which common stock was sold for additional financing, was 16.4% ($1,697/$10,325).

In 1981, it was 17.3% ($2,196/$12,683). But in 1982, it was only 12.5% ($2,689/$21,411). The explanation of the sharp fall in ROE is that during 1982, the company sold over $5.8 million worth of new common stock, thereby expanding the equity base. While the conversion cycle was generating roughly the same net profit margins of 9% each year, earnings on a per share basis did not rise proportionately with the net income of the last year because of the increase of 250,000 new shares of ownership.

Earnings per common share of ownership derives from dividing the annual net surplus by the number of outstanding shares. It represents the number of equal portions (shares) into which the equity is divided. (The ROE ratio focuses on the after-tax surplus from sales as it relates to the total equity investment. The number of shares is not relevant to this measure of profitability.) The measure of surplus attributable to a particular share or apportionment of ownership is a theoretical claim to the surplus. The percentage return to the shareowner is based on the earnings per share (EPS) divided by the price the owner paid for the share. The return too is an accounting calculation since EPS is not a measure of cash distribution. Insofar as a dividend is paid from the earnings, the owner receives part of the surplus generated. Purchasing a share of ownership means purchasing a claim to a portion of the equity which grows in part by the reinvestment of the retained surplus. And it is important to note that where preferred ownership shares are part of the equity financing, both the preferred dividend and the preferred share equity value are removed from the EPS and ROE equations. The common shareholders only have the right to the residual earnings from their investment since the preferred shareholders have a prior but limited claim to the surplus generated base on a predetermined portion of the equity.

Asset Turnover and Profitability

As discussed in the last chapter, asset turnover or the rapidity of the resource conversion cycle influences both the surplus generated and the costs and amount of financing of the conversion cycle. These ratio indicators relate components of the income statement directly with asset levels maintained in the conversion cycle as shown on the balance sheet. One might ask, "What level of assets was employed to produce the earnings during that sales period?" Surplus generated, before or after income taxes, as it relates to the level of assets employed, indirectly combines the effects of management decisions about resource use with their necessary financing costs. This *ratio of surplus to total assets* is known as ROA — the periodic surplus divided by the total assets value (equivalent to the total financing) from the balance sheet. For Haemonetics, the ROA drops from almost 10% in 1980 to 8.5% in 1981 because the total assets (marketable securities) expanded through the common stock sale more rapidly than the earned surplus.

Two points to consider when relating profits to asset utilization are (1) all ratio analysis involving the calculation of surpluses is subject to careful reflection on the effects on earnings from any changes in the accounting methods employed and (2) in a continuous conversion activity, resources are acquired for *future* use. Changes in their levels reflect changes in future productive capacity (long-life assets) and current unsold production (current assets) of the business as well as the possibility of poor asset utilization by management. Consequently, while the concept of comparing changing levels of regularly employed assets in the conversion cycle with generated surplus is a key measure, it is a gross one. More important, one should focus on the individual and influential component conversions that measure both the effects of profitability and efficiency of management in employing resources in a particular economic activity.

Current asset turnover, more specifically, the flow of cash and credit invested in inventory and receivables is measured in two conversion ratios. Each answers the question about the average time that a dollar of financing is tied up in a current asset. Together, they measure the time a dollar is invested in the current asset conversion cycle, or the *operating cycle* of an enterprise as shown in Figure 12–1. At the retail level when cash is exchanged in a sales transaction, the time frame of conversion or turnover is only the average shelf

Figure 12–1.

time between delivery and sale. If credit cards are involved, then the time is extended by the amount of time lapse between the sale and receipt of the reimbursement check from the financing company of the credit card holder. These turnover measurements indicate what minimal amount of cash has to be tied up regularly in the current asset flow in order to support a given level of sales. The level of current assets employed reflects the many management decisions about the number of products on hand, the level of financing risk, and the credit policies the company follows, all bounded by industry patterns of resource use and sales practices.

The *inventory turnover* ratio is calculated by dividing the cost of goods sold on the income statement by the inventory available at the end of the year. It is a ratio which says, that on average, a dollar of inventory turns over so many times per year. It would be low in a company building ships and high in the retail food business. It might be 100/1 or 100 times per year for the milk operation referred to earlier. This annual turnover translates into 3.6 days, based on a 360 day year. That is, on the average, you would expect to find one dollar of inventory at the end of the year for every 100 dollars worth of milk sold. In theory, the ideal conversion occurs when a new delivery of saleable resources arrives or is ready just when the last unit is sold. No excess inventory is maintained in which financing is tied up. In the real world, enterprises always have minimal stock levels of supplies and saleable goods on hand to avoid the possibility of losing a sale.

From a financial perspective, the investors' concern is that an enterprise may be financing excess inventory available for sale directly in the form of resource costs and paying extra interest on loans to finance them. If financing comes from equity capital, then it is not available for investment in other income-generating assets when tied up in excess inventory. If inventory rises in relation to COGS, the turnover slows down. On the surface, a falling inventory turnover ratio indicates that current assets are more than adequate to maintain sales levels; therefore, they are not being well managed. Consequently, the costs of the conversion cycle are not being minimized.

As a practical matter, inventory is measured on a given day, the end of the sales period. If during that period, a new line of products was being readied for sales in the near future, then the turnover ratio would drop. If the purchasing manager delayed orders of supplies and raw materials for a few days during which the ending inventory was determined, the final turnover figure might indicate that management was doing a good job.

Inventory levels are built up or reduced in anticipation of sales expectations. When the auto manufacturers plan ahead with production that anticipates sales rises, and the latter do not occur, as happened early in 1982, the industry becomes over-inventoried and production is curtailed. Inventory turnover in this industry is specifically measured by the number of days supply of cars on hand in relation to annual sales. That number will rise rapidly in the early spring, as will the level of Easter bunnies in the toy stores. New car sales are seasonally oriented as well as subject to annual model changes.

In general, since the inventory turnover ratio is calculated from the relationship between the level of past sales and the current level of resources which anticipates future sales, managerial and economic factors influencing both are usually complex and diverse. Rising inventory levels relative to past sales means increased risk in the conversion of resources. Will those resources be sold? Are they saleable? When? Those are the key thoughts of suppliers and bankers, the financiers of the operating cycle. In the spring of 1982, the auto manufacturers started their big discount programs to increase sales and to free up cash from the conversion cycle needed to pay their bankers.

As long as sales are made on company credit, the cash-to-cash conversion cycle is extended and must be financed. The *receivables turnover* ratio is the relationship between the levels of accounts receivable and sales. It represents the management of credit policies and the effectiveness of collection procedures. If longer credit terms are made available to purchasers of the company's output, the average turnover of dollars invested in the credit slows down and more financing is needed. On the other hand, discounts to induce early payment are offered to shorten the conversion cycle. A buyer may be offered 2% off if payment is made for a purchase within 10 days, on a bill due in 30 days. To the seller, this offer means 2% reduction of the sales price which is effectively traded for a savings in the financing charges. To the buyer, 2/10/30 means that 20 days of credit will cost 36% when annualized ($2\% \times 360/20$).

When making a financial analysis, one must always bear in mind that the accounts receivable of one enterprise are the payables of another enterprise. Credit extended by a supplier to finance its sales is also a source of financing someone else's conversion cycle. Designer clothes manufacturers selling to department stores during 1981 when the commercial bank interest rates were very high found that their normal receivables turnover was slowing down. Their customers financed the stock on their shelves by paying the suppliers much later than the terms of their credit sales. That condition meant the suppliers/manufacturers had to arrange more and longer financing for their sales. These manufacturers were very upset by this costly practice, but they dared not refuse to make the sales to their slow-paying customers for fear they would lose the business entirely. In effect, they became the bankers of the department store conversion cycles.

A company that is not diligent about collecting receivables loses the use of the cash generated and its earning power or pays additional interest costs for borrowed money. Large companies such as Gillette, Nabisco, and Polaroid, which provide substantial credit to their independent distributors, have to carefully manage the collection of their receivables or incur excess financing costs. For the multi-billion dollar company, reducing the average collection time by a couple of days may save millions of dollars in interest charges during a year. For small companies, the attention to collecting accounts receivable is a more obvious task, because it is often critically important to financial survival of the business.

Time IS money! The cycles of asset conversion are the cycles of financing. The cash-to-cash flow of short-life resources is traceable in the changes in the current asset composition and size. Financing must be continuously arranged to support the cycle, as measured in the turnover ratios. The total current assets flow expands and contracts with seasonal influences, economic conditions, added product lines or changes in the product mix, changing credit policy, and production scheduling. In addition poor management practices through overstocking, carrying "dead" inventory, making high-risk credit sales, and pursuing poor collection practices and billing procedures are expressed in declining ratios. Changing ratios may also indicate any number of reasons that costs and financing requirements are different from earlier experiences with the conversion cycle of an enterprise.

Another measure of the efficiency of resource utilization is the *fixed asset turnover* ratio. It compares sales of a given time period with the level of fixed assets in use at the end of the period. A strike of significant duration, for example, produces a sharp drop in this ratio, as would economic slowdowns. So would the accumulation of nonproductive assets. Operating at very high capacity with a high level of sales would produce a higher than normal utilization ratio. But when a company is expanding its production capacity, the fixed assets will be underutilized, therefore the ratio will fall. This ratio is also influenced by changes in the depreciation methodology. Accelerated depreciation policies will reduce the fixed asset value much faster than straight-line depreciation; hence utilization will appear initially higher under the former accounting method than under the latter. This ratio essentially asks the questions: "How many dollars of sales are the fixed assets producing? How does that compare with last year? With our industry?"

The all-encompassing asset utilization ratio is *total asset turnover* — sales to total assets, excluding intangible goodwill. Basically this ratio shows the total level of assets needed to produce the current level of sales. However, the balance sheet values reflect all earlier decisions and costs pertaining to resource acquisitions and financing arrangements. Expansion of fixed assets for future production are reflected in falling ratios but so is mismanagement of inventory, accumulation or credit extension, and collection. In addition, newly paid equity, which has not been spent to acquire resources, will expand cash and market securities portions of the asset base. So will recently acquired resources. All the individual asset turnover considerations are compiled in this all-encompassing general ratio.

Conversion and Liquidity Measurements

Bankers and suppliers want to know and be assured that an enterprise can pay its bills. They look at the short-term conversion cycle, in relation to the short-term debt. The *current ratio* measures the safety margin between the current assets and current liabilities. That is, if the current assets were sold at least at their accounting value, is there a good margin in excess of the current liabilities? That margin could be measured as 1.3, 2, or 3 dollars per dollar of debt. The larger the ratio, the safer the short-term creditor feels. The more critical relationship for short-term lenders, however, is known as the *quick ratio.* It is composed of only those current assets which are most liquid — cash, short-term marketable securities, and accounts receivable. It excludes inventory because it is unsold and of relatively much higher risk in the conversion cycle. The accounts receivable, however, represent the short-term debt of buyers. They are easily transferable to new owners and legally binding. In seasonally oriented industries, these receivables are often sold to financial institutions ("factored") and represent a fairly good quality investment if they come from diverse and financially reliable companies that pay their bills on time.

The quick ratio says basically that if an enterprise closes its doors tomorrow how much cash and easily marketable assets are available to cover the current liabilities. Accounts receivables are a readily saleable, low-risk asset if business conditions are seriously strained. As a practical matter, they represent a calculable flow of cash in the near future. Most smaller companies do not have marketable securities, which basically represent temporary use of excess cash flow, unless they have recently increased their major assets financed by selling stocks or bonds. These marketable securities are investments which tend to be very short-term loans of exceptionally high quality (low risk), such as U.S. Treasury Bills or commercial paper of financially sound companies and banks. Since they are highly marketable, they are considered *near cash.*

Conversion and Safety

The greater the level of debt financing, the greater the potential profitability of owners' investment because additional resources are financed with someone else's money. Long-term lenders look to the conversion cycle over time to produce the return of their principal as well as the interest. There are several perspectives involved in the position of the long-term lender that derive from the creditor status, the terms of the debt agreement, and its maker's repayment obligations. Even though long-term debt may be secured by particular assets, it is generally not in the interest of the creditors to see the conversion cycles of their debtors falter or fail. They are usually not in the business of managing resources other than financial investments. The creditors of Braniff whose long-term loans were secured by airplanes found that they could neither lease them nor sell them because of an oversupply of used airplanes on the marketplace when the company went into bankruptcy. While the creditors' security interest reserved their rights to a portion of the assets owned by the company, it did not protect the market value of these assets nor the revenue-generating capability.

Long-term lenders risk their funds to the expected long-term cash flow patterns of the conversion cycles. The design of the terms of a long-term loan agreement define future cash flow obligations of the borrower. Quarterly payments might be required, or annual payments of both principal and interest. Sometimes interest alone is paid in the first two or three years of a loan; then the principal as well as the interest is paid. This pattern would be consistent with building a new manufacturing facility and getting it into production. Only when the asset was expected to generate revenues would the principal begin to be returned. In real estate transactions, mortgage loans are sometimes made on the basis of *balloon payments*. That is a loan in which the principal is repaid at the end of the loan term while interest is paid on a regular basis. Other loans are conditioned by sinking fund arrangements to pay down part of the principal over most of the life of the loan with a significant portion paid in the last few years. Convertible bonds may have contractual repayment schedules just like any other bonds. However, they in fact may never affect the company's cash outflow if they are converted into common stock. While call provisions protect the debtor against swings in the interest rate, hence changes in the annual cost of borrowing, sinking fund and other contractual repayment structures determine future receipts for the lenders. In sum, there are innumerable variations of loan repayment schedules which may relate to the expected patterns of resource conversion and credit terms.

Since the creditors' financial position is enhanced by owners' investment, a measurement of particular and ongoing concern is the debt-to-equity ratio. Sometimes it is stated in terms of debt to total financing. This key ratio asks what percentage of dollars of equity are risked in relation to loan dollars or total investment. The riskier the conversion cycle, the more equity is expected by lenders, and the shorter the lending terms on borrowed money. With less risk in the conversion activity or the asset itself (i.e., a fully rented commercial building), greater levels of credit can be supported. However, greater levels of loans mean higher interest charges against surplus from operations and increased claims to future cash flows. At increasing risk is the generation of net surplus along with longer term liquidity, the ability to repay loans. For safety's sake, home mortgage lenders have rules of thumb about the ratio of disposable income of the borrower to the level of mortgage and tax payments which are usually collected together. Thus monthly payments cannot be at a level greater than a one-to-three or one-to-four ratio with disposable monthly income. Therefore, the level of mortgage payments capability determines the maximum level of borrowing with consideration for both the length of the loan and the interest rate.

In income statement terms, the *debt absorption capacity* of a converison cycle is measured by (1) the ability to pay annual interest from surplus generated by the conversion, and (2) the annual cash flow capability to pay fixed charges of interest and loan repayments over time. Fixed annual charges may also include long-term lease obligations as well as loan repayments. These are projected claims on the future cash flow from the assets employed which have to be met in order to stay in business. How much safety margin is there for both the annual interest obligations and the fixed charges?

Long-term debt capacity is shown on the income statement only in terms of the cost of using someone else's money. *Interest coverage* is measured by the operating income generated before the charges of interest divided by the interest cost. The greater the ratio, the safer the debt, but purely in terms of surplus generated to cover the periodic cost of debt. As the interest coverage narrows, the risk increases. Financial leverage from expanding debt utilization has its impact on the flow of operating surplus from resource conversion since rising interest costs push up the breakeven level.

Aside from the lenders' reward is the repayment of principal. The income statement only shows the relationships of surplus and costs, not cash flows. The financing of assets with debt implies the future return of original investment as well as the generation of a surplus.

Since both are at risk, safety must also be measured in the cash flow context of the ongoing conversion cycle and in context of the contracted financial obligations which support them. The cash flow measurement is called the *fixed charge coverage.* It incorporates the streams of cash flowing from operations – depreciation plus the surplus after tax. These are the major sources of funds from the conversion cycle available to cover the loan repayments. *However,* depreciation can only be considered as an annual flow from the ongoing conversion cycle if sales volume is at an accounting breakeven level. Lending for depreciable assets takes into consideration the expected pattern of depreciation flows from the conversion matched against loan repayment outflows.

The greater the equity investment in the long-life asset, the less the outflow to repay a loan. The depreciation flow does not change because of the financing mix. Its structure is based on the accounting life of the asset and the methodology to apportion the use of it on an annual basis. Here again, the investors' risks of conversion of the asset is reflected in the debt/equity level of financing which determines the future cash flow obligations. Constant monitoring of this ratio gives an indication of debt capacity and of the need to increase equity financing.

The foregoing ratio explanations are applied to the conversion cycle of Haemonetics Corporation in Table 12–1 based on figures from the balance sheets of the annual report.

The current asset turnover changed only slightly from year to year with a small increase in the average collection time. Inventory turnover indicates that as sales have increased, inventory has increased proportionately. No special explanations seem to be needed. Fixed asset turnover increase indicates that these assets are being more fully utilized. Asset utilization appears to be effective and efficient.

The current and quick ratios expanded substantially because proceeds from the new common stock issue were temporarily invested in short-term marketable securities. The excess cash will be drawn down as expansion of production facilities is completed. Thus the change in short-term liquidity results from financing transactions, not operations. If the effect of the stock financing were eliminated from the quick ratio calculation, it would have fallen to \$1.48/\$1.00 in 1982, which is still a fairly comfortable margin for the current

Table 12–1.

RATIO	1981	1982
Inventory Turnover (COGS ÷ Closing Inventory) (10,655/6,210) (14,276/8,287)	1.72 times per year	1.72 times per year
Accounts Receivable Turnover (Average) (Sales ÷ A/R) (23,954/6,276) (30,013/8,287)	3.82 times per year	3.62 times per year
Equivalent to the average collection time of (360/3.8) (360/3.65)	95 days	99 days
Fixed Asset Turnover (Sales ÷ Fixed Assets) (23,954/6,886) (30,013/8,169)	$3.48/$1.00	$3.67/$1.00
Current Ratio (Current Assets ÷ Current Liabilities) (15,465/6,711) (23,885/6,339)	$2.30/$1.00	$3.77/$1.00
Quick Ratio (Current Assets – Inventory ÷ Current Liabilities) (9,255/5,446) (16,034/6,339)	$1.70/$1.00	$2.53/$1.00
Debt Equity (9,678/12,683) (10,643/21,411)	$0.76/$1.00	$0.50/$1.00
Debt as a percentage of total financing	43%	33%
Interest Coverage (EBIT ÷ Interest) (4,228/349) (4,760/415)	12 times	11.5 times
Fixed Charge Coverage (NIAT + Depreciation ÷ Reduction in L.T. Debt) from Changes in Financial Position statement (2,765/248) (3,529/240)	11 times	14.5 times

short-term lenders. The current ratio would have remained essentially the same. As long as the inventory and accounts receivable turnover remain roughly proportional to sales, the operating cycle has not changed. One dollar of financing will pass through the conversion cycle at the same rate as the previous year. Additional financing will be needed to support additional sales based solely on resource turnover of the operating cycle. If the inventory expanded and turnover fell, due to new product introduction and slow sales of existing products in the current inventory, then the company might find it had difficulties in repaying its bank loans.

Both the cash and the marketable securities (temporary investments components of the current assets) are a result of cash flow changes and decisions about financing and asset acquisition. Haemonetics shows this perfectly. Sales and profits are based on and reflected in the levels of assets needed in the conversion. Cash and marketable securities per se are not the sales-generating assets in the cycle. By excluding these elements from the current asset ratio, one has an effective measure of changes in the operating cycle.

As to the safety of the debtor position, the debt/equity ratio improved markedly because of the sale of common stock. Both interest coverage and cash flow from operations indicate the company can absorb more debt financing with ease. However, one must carefully look at the footnotes to the balance sheet to find the schedule of future debt repayment obligations. Maybe in a few years there will be a balloon-type repayment which will sharply change the current ratio of a particular year. Those levels will be influential in determining the terms and repayment conditions of new lending agreements.

It is very important to realize that comparison of ratios from year-to-year or with other companies in a given industry may be very limited with new or rapidly growing companies. When a company acquires another which is in an entirely different business, as when Playboy, a magazine publisher, entered the hotel business, overall ratios shift reflecting the combination of conversion cycles of dramatically different economic activities. While ratios reflect patterns of industries, they also reflect resource patterns of individual enterprises. Every company has a different way of carrying on its business, though the output from the particular conversion may be very similar to the output of another company. Not only does competition change, but economic conditions in the short- and long-run also shift. Ratio analysis is anything but routine or standardized; it does provide a financial analysis framework for the various users of the information — managers, owners/shareholders, bankers, bond holders, trade creditors (suppliers), investment analysts, and others involved in the decision making and financing of resource conversion activities.

SOURCES OF FINANCIAL INFORMATION

Considerable information has been collected about the ratios in different industries. Robert Morris Associates of Philadelphia has for many years supplied the banking industry with financial profiles of over 300 lines of businesses. Dun & Bradstreet of New York has also gathered considerable information on ratios of different businesses which it collects and publishes annually. Their analyses comprise many ratios and other factors which compiled provide credit information to businesses. Publicly issued and traded bonds are "rated" by Standard & Poor's, Moody's, and Fitch & Co. They make independent and ongoing evaluations of the safety of these investments for the public, investment, and banking communities. Ratio data is published by many industries through trade groups and magazines, some large corporations and government agencies, the Small Business Administration being the most prominent.

EPILOGUE

The end of this book will hopefully be the beginning for many readers. While you will not be an expert accountant, you will have a firmer understanding of accounting terminology, a clearer perspective on standard formats of compiling financial information, and some introduction to the way it is used by managers and investors. Now pick up your annual report and see the financial story of your business or the company in which you have shares; read the business stories, especially those about financially troubled companies, that appear in the major magazines and business newspapers; analyze the investment reports, especially the longer ones, that are available from the nation's stock brokerage offices. It is in these contexts that the thoughts and concepts of the preceding pages will become more illuminating and useful. You will find that it is not dry stuff at all!

GLOSSARY

Accounts Payable. Debts owed *by* a business entity for goods and services purchased on credit. Also called *payables.*

Accounts Receivable. Debts owed *to* a business entity as a result of sales on credit; opposite of accounts payable. Also called *receivables.*

Amortization. See *Depreciation.*

Balance Sheet. The financial report of a business which shows the accounting value of resources (assets) available and their sources of financing on a given date.

Book Value. See *Net Worth.*

Breakeven. The level of sales at which revenues cover accounting costs or cash outflow. The variables that compose breakeven analysis are sales volume, unit pricing, resources and financing costs.

Capital Stock. The ownership interest in a corporation. It is divided into and represented by *shares.* Owners of shares are referred to as *shareholders* or *stockholders.* There may be different classes of ownership defined by varying rights of ownership and claims to profits. The most well-known groupings are *common* and *preferred shares.*

Cash Flow. Cash generated and paid out from the ongoing acquisition and sale of resources of a business entity.

Collateral. Something of value which secures or backs up a loan agreement.

Common Stock. A class of ownership participation representing the highest level of financing risk.

Consolidation. The combining of accounting records of separate entities into one legal entity.

Conversion Cycle. The flow from acquisition to sale of resources of an economic entity.

Corporation. A legal entity or person with a life separate from its owners. Money contributed by owners to finance the corporation is *capital stock.*

Cost of Goods Sold. Those costs in manufacturing, such as labor, materials and energy, directly related to a unit of production. In retailing, the cost of purchases. These costs are also referred to as *direct costs*.

Depletion. See *Depreciation*.

Depreciation. The periodic allocation of a part of the original cost of a long-life resource consumed in production. It is a cost category on the profit and loss statement. *Depreciation* specifically applies to tangible resources such as equipment and buildings. Land does not depreciate. *Depletion* applies to natural resources such as oil, ore, gravel and clay. Intangible resources such as the value of patents or franchises are *amortized*.

Dividends. The distribution of profit or return of original investment to owners of a business.

EBIT. Acronym for Earnings Before Interest and Taxes. See *Operating Income*.

Equity. Owners' financing of a business enterprise.

FIFO. Acronym for First-in, First-out. An accounting method for determining the cost of goods sold during a given time period. It is based on purchase costs at the *beginning* of an accounting period.

Financial Leverage. The use of fixed-cost financing to increase the available amount of resources employed by an enterprise. Potential gains and losses from these resources increases the risk of and reward to the owners' investment.

Goodwill. An intangible resource (asset) whose value equals the difference between the purchase price and the net worth of an acquired business.

Income Statement. The financial report which shows the value of sales and resources and the financial costs to produce them during a specific time period.

Individual Proprietorship. A business owned by a single individual and not incorporated as a separate entity.

Inventory. The short-life resources available for production, those that are in production and products available for sale.

Liabilities. Actual or potential debts and obligations arising from a business transaction.

LIFO. Acronym for Last-in, First-out. An accounting method for determining the cost of goods sold during a given time period. It is based on purchase costs at the *end* of the accounting period.

Liquidity. The availability of cash to meet actual and pending debt obligations or contingencies.

Marketable Securities. Short-term low-risk investments, such as U.S. Treasury bills and commercial paper, which are easily saleable.

Mark-up. The difference between the sales price and the direct cost of a product or service.

Net Worth. The difference between the accounting value of the resources of an entity and the debt owed by the entity. Also referred to as *owners' equity* and (net) *book value.*

Notes Payable. Written promises to pay given sums on defineable dates. They usually bear a specific rate of interest.

Notes Receivable. Same transaction as the above, held by the recipient.

Operating Costs. The costs of long-life production and organizational resources shown on the income statement. Some of the main groupings are general and administrative, marketing and sales, research and development, maintenance, leases, depreciation or depletion, accounting and legal.

Operating Profit. The same as Earnings Before Interest and Taxes (EBIT); sales revenues less cost of goods sold and operating costs of the normal and ongoing business activities. Financing costs and gains are excluded.

Paid-in Capital. Investment money paid into a corporation by owners and exchanged for shares of ownership.

Par Value. A nominal and often arbitrary value placed on the common stock of a corporation. Preferred stock more often than not has a par value equivalent to its original issue price. It establishes the limit of the liability of the shareholder.

Partnership. A business entity in which there are two or more co-owners. Profits and losses are generally shared in relationship to percentage of individual investment. Partnerships may be *general* or *limited.* In the former, each partner has unlimited liability for all the obligations of the business. A limited partnership combines both general and limited partners whereby the latter have a limited liability in accordance with the partnership agreement.

Prepaid Expenses. Costs of short-life (less than a year) resources which are paid for in advance of their use, for example, insurance and rent. They exclude purchases for production or inventory.

Profit Margin. The percent of a dollar of sales that represents the surplus or profit generated by the sale. It may be before or after taxes.

Ratio Analysis. Financial analysis that deals with the relationships between different components on the income statement and balance sheet. It provides measurements of liquidity, efficient use of resources, financial leverage and profitability.

Retained Earnings. Earnings or profits of a business entity which have not been paid out to shareholders. Also referred to as *reinvested* or *accumulated earnings.*

Return on Assets (ROA). The relationship between profit during a given accounting period and the total investment in resources (assets).

Return on Equity/Investment (ROE) or (ROI). The relationship between profit (before or after taxes) during a given accounting period and the overall owners' investment.

Risk. The possibility or probability that what is expected to occur does not in fact occur. With investment decisions, personal or corporate, the greater the possibility that resources may not produce profits, the higher the risk attached to the investment, i.e. drilling for oil.

Salvage Value. Estimated resale value of a tangible long-life resource at the end of its estimated productive life. Often a matter of estimating future *scrap value.*

Secured Investment. See *Collateral.*

Serial Redemption. The gradual retirement of a bond issue in accordance with an established series of due dates.

Shareholders. The owners of shares or stock of a corporation. Same as *stockholders.*

Sinking Fund. A method of retiring bonds by which a certain amount of cash is set aside in a fund annually to purchase the company's bonds.

Statement of Changes in Financial Position. A financial report which shows the changes in the balance sheet items that have occurred between two points in time. Useful in determining changes in liquidity and future cashflows.

Subchapter S Corporation. A certain type of small corporation allowed by the Internal Revenue Code to be taxed as a partnership, thereby passing on the income tax effects to individual owners. Also known as *"S" Corporation.*

Surplus. The difference between cost and price of goods and services sold. The same as *profit*.

Useful Life. An estimate of the time that a long-life resource will be usefully employed in a business activity. It is the basis for calculating annual depreciation charges.

Zero Coupon Bonds. Bonds which do not pay interest before their redemption dates. Interest, compounded annually, accumulates on the sales prices of these bonds during their lifetimes, and is paid in a lumpsum at the redemption date. For example, a $1,000 bond due at the end of 10 years has a current price or present value of $386, given a compound annual interest rate of 10%.

INDEX

INDEX

DATE DUE

NO 13 '87			
JUL 14 1988			
DE 03 '01			

DEMCO 38-297